WING CRUSH

WING CRUSH

100
EPIC RECIPES
FOR YOUR GRILL
OR SMOKER

PAULA STACHYRA
CREATOR OF QUEEN OF THE GRILL

PAGE STREET
PUBLISHING CO.

First published in 2022 by

Page Street Publishing Co.

27 Congress Street, Suite 1511

Salem, MA 01970

www.pagestreetpublishing.com

Distributed by Macmillan, sales in Canada by The Canadian Manda Group.

26 25 24 23 22   1 2 3 4 5

ISBN-13: 978-1-64567-550-1

ISBN-10: 1-64567-550-5

Library of Congress Control Number: 2021940659

Cover and book design by Rosie Stewart for Page Street Publishing Co.

Photography by Paula Stachyra

Printed and bound in the United States of America

DEDICATION

For my husband, my family and my late, great grilling
sidekick dog, Sandy

CONTENTS

INTRODUCTION

Ain't no thing but a chicken wing. Do you love chicken wings? Are you a grill enthusiast? If the answer is yes to both, you've come to the right place. Chicken wings have become one of the most popular foods for major sporting events, social gatherings with friends and family, late-night cravings, weeknight meals and as a restaurant menu item—and with good reason, in my opinion!

It's no secret that I have a love affair with chicken wings. I may or may not be a wingaholic. They're on my weekly rotation, sometimes twice a week. I enjoy exploring flavors and coming up with creative and innovative recipes, and I started sharing them on my Instagram page every Wednesday with the hashtag #WingCrushWednesday, WCW for short. I thought it would be fun to post some out-of-the-box recipes and motivate others to do so as well. Fast forward to today, WCW has become something people look forward to, associate me with, use to tag me in their creations and when they re-create my recipes and are excited to see what I come up with next.

My journey with grilling started well before then, however. I've been drawn to it since the family camping trips we took in my childhood, when my mom would make the best-tasting wings with just a handful of ingredients. Most of the time everyone was gathered around the grill, connecting over food and creating fond memories. As I got older, I eventually took over the family grilling duties, which is how I learned to grill on propane and charcoal.

I became serious about grilling about 6 years ago when I got my first charcoal grill, an Original Weber® Kettle. The first meal I grilled to break it in? You guessed it—chicken wings! I grilled almost daily, which led me to learn how to smoke the perfect ribs, pork butt, brisket, tri-tip and spatchcocked chicken, among other dishes. A few years later, I added a Traeger® pellet grill to my arsenal and challenged myself to learn new ways to grill and perfect my love for grilling using both grills. Once I had all the basic knowledge and I knew what worked and what didn't, I started creating some innovative and unique recipes.

All that led me to a live television appearance where I showcased some of my burger recipes grilling on my Weber charcoal grill for National Cheeseburger Day in 2019. The biggest moment in my journey was when three of my recipes, at different times, were featured on Rachael Ray's magazine's Instagram page. Since then, I've become an ambassador for brands, worked with a handful of companies doing recipe development and was featured in Arteflame's "Women of the Grill" newsletter.

I've tested different methods and have perfected how to make the ultimate crispy, crunchy, tender, juicy and finger-lickin' good wings on every type of grill, from gas and pellet to kamado style and charcoal. In the following pages you will learn those tips and tricks, along with information on buying, splitting, stuffing and preparing chicken wings. Then, we will put that knowledge to work with my epic chicken wing recipes! Your chicken wing game will be taken to the next level.

There is a recipe for everyone in this vast collection. The best part? They are simple to make, many use ingredients you probably already have and you don't need any special commercial equipment to make them. Got a grill? Got an oven? Perfect, let's make some wings! I am excited to share them with you and I hope you enjoy them as much as I do.

This book is a labor of love for me, and a dream come true. I love wings, grilling and sharing my knowledge and passion with all of you, and I can only hope you love this book as much as I do. Also, I may or may not be responsible for the chicken wing shortage at my local grocery store. Oops!

WINGS 101

Welcome to Wings 101, where I'll teach you everything you need to know about chicken wings, including how to cut, stuff and prepare them. You'll also learn the best tips and tricks to serve crispy, tender and juicy wings. In the end, you will become a Wingmaster! Let's get started.

ANATOMY OF A WING

Chicken wings (I also refer to them as flappers) are made up of three parts: the tips, flats and drumettes.

Tip
The tip is the tiny, pointy piece at the end. It has little to no meat and is just skin, bone and cartilage. Chicken wing tips are perfect to freeze and use for chicken stock.

Flat (Wingette)
The flat (wingette) is the part of the wing that is between the elbow and tip. There are two thin bones that run parallel to each other down the length of the flat. This is the tender dark meat portion of the wing.

Drumette
The drumette looks like a mini drumstick and is the part that is attached to the body (breast) of the chicken and runs from shoulder to elbow. There's one main bone in the middle and some joints and cartilage on both ends. One end is round and meaty, and the other end has a handle. The drumette has a higher ratio of meat to skin in comparison to the flat and has a texture that is like white meat.

BUYING CHICKEN WINGS

Should you buy whole or split wings?
It's all about preference and there is no right or wrong answer. In the end it comes down to time and money. You'll usually save money by buying whole wings and cutting them up yourself (or keeping them whole if you prefer), but you'll save time by buying split wings. Which is more important to you?

Tip: If you're planning on purchasing fresh wings before a big game or event, like the Super Bowl, I highly recommend stocking up the week before, as some stores may have limited supplies the day before or the day of. Simply freeze them and then thaw them in the fridge overnight.

How many chicken wings should you buy?
This will vary based on if there are other things on the menu, and if you've got big eaters, you may want to make more. On average you want to account for ½ pound (227 g) of wings per person, so 2 pounds (908 g) for 4 people, for example.

HOW TO CUT CHICKEN WINGS

So, you've got whole wings in front of you and need to separate them? Perfect, you saved money and it's easy to do. You'll be a master in no time. You need a good sharp knife (I use my Dalstrong © Chef's knife for this job) and a cutting board.

Place the wing on the cutting board and stretch it out (see photo below). You'll see the three parts of the wing: the tip, flat and drumette. Flip the wing over so that you can easily see the joints. Cut the tip cleanly with one cut right through the joint. Set the tips aside and freeze them to make stock. Next, cut through the two joints where the wing naturally bends. Push the knife through. If you have some resistance, wiggle the knife a little and when you feel less resistance, push the knife down. That's it, you're done! You can finish off with the chicken dance.

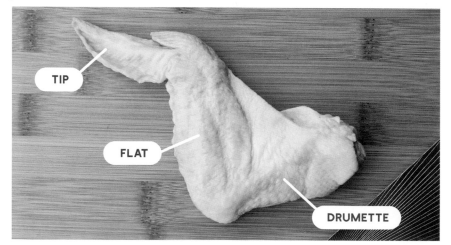

HOW TO STUFF CHICKEN WINGS

Stuffed wings? WHAAATTT? Yes, it's a thing and absolutely possible without deboning the drumettes and flats. This requires a little bit of time and effort, but it's all worth it in the end. It will blow your mind. The possibilities and creativity are endless with fillings.

To stuff wings, loosen the skin around the drumette and flat areas on the meatier side opposite of the bone with your fingers or thumb to create a pocket that can be stuffed. Fill each wing with about ½ teaspoon or more of filling. Push the filling as far down as possible. You don't want to overstuff, so be sure to leave some room to close the flap. Flipping stuffed wings on the grill is not recommended. It's not unusual for some filling to come out during the grilling process. See the Wings Gone Wild chapter (page 149) for some crave-worthy stuffed wing recipes.

Stuffing the pocket with filling

HOW TO PREPARE CHICKEN WINGS

There are a couple of ways to prepare wings prior to grilling, smoking or baking, from simple brines and marinades to dry rubs to achieve crispy skin. I'm going to share some of the best tips and tricks for these methods. To start, go ahead and remove the wings from the package and thoroughly pat them dry with a paper towel to remove any excess liquid and moisture. You will have to repeat this step once you remove the wings from a brine or marinade. Doing so will promote browning and crispy skin. If you skip this step, any moisture left on the skin will create steam during the cooking process and you'll end up with less than crispy skin.

Brine/Marinade

Brining will take your wings to the next level with only a few ingredients. Simple, right? The result: tender and juicy chicken wings. This process helps prevent the meat from drying out, which is important for BBQ and smoking. There are many brine recipes out there, but my favorite is dill pickle juice. I also suggest beer, water, salt and sugar, buttermilk or jalapeño pickling juice for some heat. Add some of your favorite dry ingredients to the brine for added flavor. Make sure to pick a brine with flavors you want to appear in the final product. Brine the wings for at least 3 hours and up to 24 hours for best results. The longer the wings brine, the more flavor is absorbed into the skin and meat.

While brining is for moisture, marinating is primarily about flavor. Marinades usually contain some acid component, which helps break down and tenderize the protein. The meat will be infused with the flavors of the marinade, whether that's a sauce, spices, herbs or some other flavor enhancers. You need to be careful not to marinate the wings too long because the acidity will start breaking down the protein too much, leaving you with a not-so-pleasant, mushy-like texture. For best results, marinate wings for 2 to 12 hours, or a minimum of 30 minutes if you're in a rush. Make sure to always refrigerate when brining or marinating, and discard the liquid when you're done.

Dry Rub/Crispy Skin

Whether you combine ingredients to make a rub or use your favorite prepared rub, always season the wings liberally—that will bring out their flavor.

Let's talk about cornstarch. It's the secret to crispy wings. If you want the ultimate crispy, crunchy wings, add some cornstarch to the rub before seasoning the wings. The most basic rub starts with salt, pepper, garlic powder, paprika and cayenne for heat. This book is full of rub recipes that are simple to make with ingredients you probably already have in your pantry.

Alternatively, toss the wings in salt and cornstarch and place them on a baking/cooling rack on top of a lined baking sheet, making sure they are evenly spaced. Leave them uncovered in the fridge for at least an hour, ideally overnight. This will help draw out moisture and dry out the skin for that sought-after crispy texture. Once you are ready to cook the wings, take them out of the fridge and let them come to room temperature for 20 to 30 minutes.

Congratulations! You just graduated with honors from Wingmaster University.

GRILLING AND COOKING TECHNIQUES

Now that we have gone through Wings 101, it's time for the fun part: grilling and cooking! I'll walk you through setting up, managing temperature and learning how to cook perfect wings every time on some of the most popular types of grills on the market. No grill? No problem; I'll show you how to bake the most incredible wings in an oven. Use the following methods and techniques and apply them to any recipe in the book based on the equipment you are using.

Chicken wings should be cooked to a minimum internal temperature of 165°F (75°C). I prefer them a little more well done and take them up to 190°F (90°C). Check for doneness by inserting an instant-read thermometer into the thickest part of the meat, being careful to avoid the bone.

You want to set the grill temperature to at least 350°F (180°C), which seems to be the magic number to achieve tender, juicy and perfect wings every time.

To sauce or not to sauce, that is the question. If you're going to sauce your wings, make sure to do so in the last 5 to 10 minutes of cooking, allowing the sauce time to caramelize. You can also toss them in sauce once you remove the wings and are ready to serve them. Keep in mind that most BBQ sauces contain sugar. Sugar burns at about 265°F (130°C), so if you're grilling above that temperature, the sugars in the sauce will burn and leave an unpleasant flavor.

If you are going to use a baking sheet to cook the wings, the key to get them crispy is to place them on a baking/cooling rack on top of the lined baking sheet, evenly spaced. This will ensure the heat circulates all around the wings and any liquid released will drip. The wings will roast instead of steam.

PELLET GRILLS (SUCH AS THE LOUISIANA GRILLS® 1200 BLACK LABEL AND TRAEGER)

Pellet grills will be the easiest to set up and maintain temperature. First, make sure to check that the hopper is full of pellets. Next, set the temperature to at least 350°F (180°C), unless otherwise stated in a recipe. Place the wings directly on the grill grates and grill for 40 minutes or until they reach a minimum internal temperature of 165°F (75°C), flipping them halfway through the cooking time. All pellet grills have hot spots, so be sure to rotate the wings for even cooking. Avoid opening the lid too frequently, as this will reduce the temperature of the grill and prolong the cooking time. If you want more of a crispy skin, increase the grill temperature to 400°F (200°C) during the last 15 minutes, turning occasionally until the skin is a dark, golden color or to your liking. For an extra kiss of smoke, start the grill at 180°F (80°C) for the first 30 minutes, then increase the temperature to 350°F (180°C).

KAMADO-STYLE GRILLS (SUCH AS THE BIG GREEN EGG)

I set up my kamado-style grill for indirect cooking by filling a load of lump charcoal and opening the top and bottom vents all the way. Light the charcoal and keep the lid open for about 10 minutes. Put soaked, drained wood chips on top of the coals for a smoky flavor (optional). Install the plate setter to avoid charring, flare-ups and singed arm hair. Keep the lid closed until the temperature increases and reaches 325°F (165°C) to 350°F (180°C). Adjust the top and bottom vents to maintain, lower or increase the temperature. Grill the wings for 30 to 40 minutes or until they reach a minimum internal temperature of 165°F (75°C), flipping them once or twice.

WEBER KETTLE GRILL

Before preheating the grill for indirect cooking, make sure that the dampers on the bottom are completely open. Remove the top grilling grate and fill the chimney starter halfway with charcoal and light. Alternatively, arrange the charcoal into a pyramid shape or minion method. The minion method works by creating a circle around your charcoal grate with lump charcoal/briquettes and then adding lit charcoal/briquettes into the middle of the unlit charcoal/briquettes. Once the charcoal has ashed over, evenly dump or spread it in the middle. Put soaked, drained wood chips on top of the coals or in a smoker box for a smoky flavor (optional). Place the cooking grate back and close the lid making sure that the lid vent is completely open. Once the grill reaches 325ºF (165ºC) to 350ºF (180ºC), you can adjust the bottom damper and lid vent to maintain, lower or increase the temperature. Place the wings on the outer rim of the grate with the charcoal in the middle. This creates the perfect environment for them to be grilled to perfection. Grill the wings for 30 to 40 minutes or until they reach a minimum internal temperature of 165ºF (75ºC), flipping them halfway through the cooking time. If you want crispier skin, move the wings to the middle (direct heat side) of the grill, turning occasionally, until the skin is a dark, golden color or to your liking.

WEBER SMOKEY MOUNTAIN COOKER™

Set up the grill for direct cooking. You will not need to use the water pan. Make sure the top and bottom vents are fully open and the charcoal chamber is empty. Light a chimney full of charcoal and dump it into the charcoal chamber once you see gray ash just starting to form at the top of the chimney. Put soaked, drained wood chips on top of the coals or in a smoker box for a smoky flavor (optional). Once the temperature reaches 325ºF (165ºC) to 350ºF (180ºC), adjust the bottom vents to about half open and keep the top one fully open. Place the wings directly on the grill grates and grill for about 1 hour or until they reach a minimum internal temperature of 165ºF (75ºC), flipping them halfway through the cooking time. Adjust the bottom vents during the cooking process to maintain, lower or increase the temperature.

OVEN BAKING

Start by preheating the oven to at least 400ºF (200ºC) or 425ºF (220ºC). If you are looking to achieve the best crispy, oven-baked wings, baking them at a higher temperature is the trick. If you are baking them lower than 400ºF (200ºC), the skin won't be as crispy. Place an oven-safe baking/cooling rack on top of a lined baking sheet and place the wings on the rack, evenly spaced. This will ensure that the heat circulates all around the wings and any liquid released drips away. The wings will roast instead of steam. Bake for about 45 minutes or until they reach a minimum internal temperature of 165ºF (75ºC). If you don't have a baking rack, simply place the wings on a parchment paper–lined sheet, flipping them halfway through the cooking time. Make sure to keep an eye on the wings so that the seasoning doesn't burn. You're looking for a crispy and golden-brown finish.

MUST-HAVE CLASSICS

When you think of classic chicken wing recipes, what comes to mind? Most people will say Buffalo, which has become a go-to flavor. I've compiled some of the most popular recipes that are sought after at a party, game day or those nights when you are simply craving wings. Some of my favorites include Sandy's Smokehouse (page 27), Hot Stripe Ranch (page 37) and Fresh Chimichurri (page 44). From sweet, smoky, sticky, spicy and everything in between, there's a recipe for everyone.

BEST EVER BUFFALO

These are the BEST Buffalo chicken wings you'll ever make! Buffalo, New York is the home of the hot wing, dating back to 1964. This flavor has gained such popularity that most restaurants feature them as a main menu item, and they are a go-to flavor for most people. These wings are crispy, saucy and perfect for game day, an informal party or those nights when you simply want to pig out on Buffalo wings paired with my blue cheese dipping sauce.

SERVINGS: 4

2 lb (907 g) chicken wings, tips removed, drums and flats separated

1 tsp garlic powder

1 tsp onion powder

1 tsp paprika

½ tsp cayenne pepper

Salt and pepper, to taste

1 tsp cornstarch

BLUE CHEESE DIPPING SAUCE

⅓ cup (80 ml) sour cream

¼ cup (60 ml) mayonnaise

½ cup (56 g) crumbled blue cheese

1 tbsp (15 ml) white vinegar

1 tbsp (9 g) minced garlic

1 tbsp (15 ml) freshly squeezed lemon juice

Salt and pepper, to taste

BUFFALO SAUCE

½ cup (120 g) Frank's RedHot® Original

1 tbsp (15 ml) honey

1 tbsp (15 ml) white vinegar

4 tbsp (56 g) unsalted butter

FOR SERVING

Celery sticks

With a paper towel, pat the wings dry. In a small bowl, combine the garlic powder, onion powder, paprika, cayenne, salt, pepper and cornstarch. Sprinkle the prepared rub over the wings, coating evenly.

Prepare the dipping sauce. In a medium bowl, combine the sour cream, mayonnaise, crumbled blue cheese, white vinegar, garlic, lemon juice, salt and pepper. Cover and refrigerate until ready to serve.

Preheat the grill or smoker to 350°F (180°C), indirect heat.

Grill the wings for 40 minutes or until they reach a minimum internal temperature of 165°F (75°C), or 190°F (90°C) if you like them well-done. Flip them halfway through the cooking time. To crisp the skin, move the wings to the direct heat side of the grill, turning occasionally, until the skin is dark golden or to your liking.

Meanwhile, prepare the sauce. In a small saucepan over medium-low heat, whisk together the hot sauce, honey and vinegar. Bring it to a simmer, then stir in the butter. Cook until the butter is melted and slightly reduced, about 2 minutes.

Transfer the wings to a bowl and toss with the Buffalo Sauce until completely coated. Plate the wings and serve them with the Blue Cheese Dipping Sauce and celery sticks.

LEMON PEPPER

These Lemon Pepper chicken wings are crispy, bursting with bright lemon and a spicy bite of black pepper flavor tossed in melted butter! Once you try them, they will be a frequent go-to and quickly become a huge hit with your family and friends! They are tender, juicy and mild enough that everyone can enjoy them. If you're crunched for time, feel free to use your favorite lemon pepper seasoning instead of making your own.

SERVINGS: 4

LEMON PEPPER SEASONING

½ cup (50 g) lemon zest (4–5 lemons)

1 tbsp (14 g) coarse salt

2½ tbsp (16 g) freshly ground black pepper

2 tsp (6 g) garlic powder

1 tbsp (7 g) onion powder

2 lb (907 g) chicken wings, tips removed, drums and flats separated

LEMON BUTTER SAUCE

4 tbsp (56 g) unsalted butter, melted

2 tbsp (30 ml) freshly squeezed lemon juice

½ tsp black pepper

FOR SERVING

2 tbsp (8 g) chopped parsley

Lemon wedges

Ranch or blue cheese dressing

Carrot and celery sticks

Preheat the toaster oven/oven to the lowest setting. Line a baking sheet with parchment paper.

Make the seasoning. Using a zester, zest the lemons (only the yellow part of the peel) onto the lined baking sheet. Spread the zest evenly and bake low and slow until the zest is completely dried, 1 to 2 hours (check after 30 minutes). Transfer the lemon zest to a small bowl and, using the back of a spoon, crush until it reaches the desired texture. Alternatively, grind the dried lemon zest in a spice grinder. Mix in the salt, pepper, garlic powder and onion powder.

With a paper towel, pat the wings dry. Sprinkle about 1½ to 2 tablespoons (22 to 29 g) of the prepared rub over the wings, coating evenly.

Preheat the grill or smoker to 350°F (180°C), indirect heat.

Grill the wings for 40 minutes or until they reach a minimum internal temperature of 165°F (75°C), or 190°F (90°C) if you like them well done, flipping them halfway through the cooking time. To crisp the skin, move the wings to the direct heat side of the grill and turn them occasionally, until the skin is dark golden or to your liking.

Meanwhile, prepare the sauce. In a large bowl, stir together the warm melted butter, lemon juice and pepper. Add the wings and toss until completely coated. Plate the wings and garnish them with parsley. Serve them with lemon wedges, ranch or blue cheese dressing and carrot and celery sticks.

GARLIC PARMESAN

These wings will be the life of the party! They are a must-have on game day, at a party or anytime you're craving wings. The rich, buttery, garlicky Parmesan sauce combined with the mouthwatering roasted garlic dipping sauce will have you licking your fingers and smacking your lips. These are a game changer.

SERVINGS: 4

2 lb (907 g) chicken wings, tips removed, drums and flats separated

1 tbsp (8 g) paprika

2 tbsp (17 g) garlic powder

½ tsp cayenne pepper

Salt and pepper, to taste

ROASTED GARLIC PARMESAN DIPPING SAUCE

2 large cloves garlic, peeled

1 tbsp (15 ml) extra-virgin olive oil

½ cup (120 ml) Caesar dressing

¼ cup (25 g) grated Parmesan cheese

¼ cup (60 ml) mayonnaise

GARLIC PARMESAN SAUCE

½ cup (112 g) unsalted butter, melted

3 cloves garlic, minced

½ cup (50 g) grated Parmesan cheese

½ tsp black pepper

2 tbsp (8 g) chopped fresh parsley

FOR SERVING

Grated Parmesan cheese

Roasted Garlic Parmesan Dipping Sauce

Carrot and celery sticks

With a paper towel, pat the wings dry. In a small bowl, combine the paprika, garlic powder, cayenne, salt and pepper. Sprinkle the prepared rub over the wings, coating evenly.

Preheat the grill or smoker to 350°F (180°C), indirect heat.

To roast the garlic for the dipping sauce, place the peeled garlic in a small ramekin or baking dish and pour in the olive oil. Cover tightly with foil. Place on the grill grates and cook for about 25 minutes or until the garlic softens. Let the garlic cool slightly and mash it with a fork until smooth. In a small bowl, combine the Caesar dressing, Parmesan cheese, mayonnaise and roasted garlic. Refrigerate until ready to serve.

Grill the wings for 40 minutes or until they reach a minimum internal temperature of 165°F (75°C), or 190°F (90°C) if you like them well done, flipping them halfway through the cooking time. To crisp the skin, move the wings to the direct heat side of the grill, turning occasionally, until the skin is dark golden or to your liking.

Meanwhile, prepare the sauce. In a large bowl, stir together the warm melted butter, garlic, Parmesan cheese, pepper and parsley. Add the wings and toss until completely coated. Plate the wings and sprinkle some more Parmesan cheese on top. Serve them with the Roasted Garlic Parmesan Dipping Sauce and carrot and celery sticks.

* See image on page 24 (shown on the bottom).

SANDY'S SMOKE-HOUSE

These chicken wings will be legendary in your home. They are seasoned to perfection, smoked low and slow and smothered in a mouthwatering spiced butter sauce. You'll be the MVP at any party or at the dinner table. These are a game day and party favorite. Keep the napkins handy. These wings are named after my late, great grilling sidekick dog, Sandy, who always followed the smoke trail hoping something would drop off the grill for her to snack on.

SERVINGS: 4

2 lb (907 g) chicken wings, tips removed, drums and flats separated

RUB
2¼ tsp (6 g) paprika

2 tsp (8 g) brown sugar

1½ tsp (4 g) garlic powder

1½ tsp (4 g) onion powder

1½ tsp (2 g) dried thyme

1½ tsp (2 g) dried oregano

½ tsp dried sage

½ tsp cayenne pepper

¾ tsp black pepper

¾ tsp white pepper

1 tbsp (18 g) salt, or to taste

SMOKEHOUSE SAUCE
1 cup (224 g) unsalted butter, melted

½ cup (120 ml) Frank's RedHot Original

½ tsp smoked paprika

¼ cup (29 g) Old Bay® seasoning (or use my recipe page 50)

Juice of 1 lemon

Salt and pepper, to taste

FOR SERVING
2 tbsp (12 g) chopped green onion

Ranch or blue cheese dressing

Carrot and celery sticks

With a paper towel, pat the wings dry. Place the wings in a shallow dish or resealable plastic bag. In a small bowl, combine all of the ingredients of the rub. Sprinkle the prepared rub over the wings, coating evenly. Cover and refrigerate for a minimum of 2 hours or overnight (the longer the better for best flavor results).

Preheat the grill or smoker to 225°F (110°C), indirect heat.

Smoke the wings for 1 hour, flipping them halfway through the cooking time.

Meanwhile, prepare the sauce. In a medium bowl, whisk together all of the ingredients for the sauce.

Remove the wings from the grill, transfer to a bowl, and increase the temperature to 350°F (180°C), indirect heat. Pour half of the Smokehouse Sauce over the wings and toss until completely coated. Place them back on the grill grates for about 20 minutes or until they reach a minimum internal temperature of 165°F (75°C), or 190°F (90°C) if you like them well done. To crisp the skin, move the wings to the direct heat side of the grill, turning occasionally, until the skin is dark golden or to your liking.

Transfer the wings to a bowl and toss with the remaining Smokehouse Sauce until completely coated. Plate the wings, garnish with the green onion, and serve them with ranch or blue cheese dressing for dipping and carrot and celery sticks.

* See image on page 24 (shown on the top).

KICKIN' CAJUN

This is one of my favorite dry rubs for chicken wings! These Cajun wings are crispy, juicy and have the perfect amount of heat. Once you make the first batch, you'll be making them over and over again. Adjust the salt level to your preference and serve them with the Cajun Avocado Crema for dipping. This recipe makes a lot of seasoning, so you'll definitely have some left over for the next batch or to use in your favorite dish.

SERVINGS: 4

2 lb (907 g) chicken wings, tips removed, drums and flats separated

3 tbsp (25 g) paprika

2 tbsp (17 g) garlic powder

1 tbsp (7 g) onion powder

1 tbsp (5 g) cayenne pepper

1 tsp red pepper flakes

½ tbsp (2 g) dried thyme

½ tbsp (2 g) dried oregano

1 tbsp (8 g) chili powder

1 tbsp (8 g) black pepper

1 tsp white pepper

½ tbsp (7 g) kosher salt, or to taste

CAJUN AVOCADO CREMA

1 ripe avocado

¼ cup (60 ml) Greek yogurt, sour cream or ranch

2 cloves garlic

¼ cup (4 g) chopped cilantro

2 tbsp (30 ml) fresh lime juice

1 tsp Cajun rub (page 94)

FOR SERVING

2 tbsp (12 g) chopped green onion

Cajun Avocado Crema

Carrot and celery sticks

With a paper towel, pat the wings dry. In a small bowl, combine the paprika, garlic powder, onion powder, cayenne, red pepper flakes, thyme, oregano, chili powder, black pepper, white pepper and salt. Sprinkle about 3 tablespoons (18 g) of the prepared rub over the wings, coating evenly.

Preheat the grill or smoker to 350°F (180°C), indirect heat.

Grill the wings for 40 minutes or until they reach a minimum internal temperature of 165°F (75°C), or 190°F (90°C) if you like them well done, flipping them halfway through the cooking time. To crisp the skin, move the wings to the direct heat side of the grill, turning occasionally, until the skin is dark golden or to your liking.

Meanwhile, prepare the dipping sauce. In a blender, place the avocado, yogurt, garlic, cilantro, lime juice and Cajun rub. Process until completely smooth.

Plate the wings and garnish them with green onion. Serve them with the Cajun Avocado Crema dipping sauce and carrot and celery sticks.

NASHVILLE HOT

It's getting Nashville hot in here! These finger-licking good chicken wings are juicy and smothered in a Nashville-style hot sauce for a kick of cayenne heat with a hint of brown sugar sweetness. Cool your palate (should you even want to) with a side of ranch dip. Serve them with some traditional bread and butter pickles, Texas toast and plenty of napkins on the side.

SERVINGS: 4

2 lb (907 g) chicken wings, tips removed, drums and flats separated

¼ cup (60 ml) dill pickle juice/brine

2 tbsp (28 g) brown sugar

3 tbsp (16 g) cayenne pepper

1 tsp red pepper flakes

1 tsp garlic powder

1 tsp paprika

1 tsp chili powder

1 tsp kosher salt

1 tsp cornstarch

1 tsp honey

NASHVILLE HOT SAUCE

½ cup (120 ml) oil

Remaining dry rub

FOR SERVING

A drizzle of honey

2 pieces Texas toast

Pickle slices

Ranch or blue cheese dressing

With a paper towel, pat the wings dry. Place the wings in a shallow dish or resealable plastic bag. Pour the pickle juice over the top and try to ensure all the wings are submerged. Cover and refrigerate for 1 to 4 hours (the longer the better for best flavor results).

Remove the wings from the refrigerator and pat dry with a paper towel. Discard the brine.

In a small bowl, combine the brown sugar, cayenne, red pepper flakes, garlic powder, paprika, chili powder and salt. Sprinkle enough of the prepared rub over the wings so that they are coated evenly. Top with the cornstarch and toss. Set aside any remaining dry rub for the Nashville Hot Sauce.

Preheat the grill or smoker to 350°F (180°C), indirect heat.

Grill the wings for 40 minutes or until they reach a minimum internal temperature of 165°F (75°C), or 190°F (90°C) if you like them well done, flipping them halfway through the cooking time. To crisp the skin, move the wings to the direct heat side of the grill, turning occasionally, until the skin is dark golden or to your liking.

Meanwhile, prepare the sauce. In a small saucepan, heat the oil over medium heat. Add in the remaining dry rub, whisking until smooth. Simmer for 2 to 3 minutes. Set aside.

Transfer the wings to a bowl and toss with the Nashville Hot Sauce until completely coated. Plate the wings and drizzle with the honey. Serve them with Texas toast, pickles, ranch or blue cheese dressing and plenty of napkins.

BACKYARD BBQ 'BAMA

These Backyard BBQ 'Bama chicken wings are sure to be a smokin' good time! The smoky flavors are a combination of smoked paprika, chili powder and chipotle powder finished off with the famous Alabama White Sauce that delivers the magic. One bite will make you want to scream and shout! Every backyard BBQ chef should have this recipe in their arsenal.

SERVINGS: 4

2 lb (907 g) chicken wings, tips removed, drums and flats separated

1 tsp smoked paprika

1 tbsp (14 g) brown sugar

1 tbsp (14 g) granulated sugar

1 tsp chili powder

1 tsp onion powder

1 tsp garlic powder

¼ tsp chipotle powder

Salt and pepper, to taste

ALABAMA WHITE SAUCE

1 cup (240 ml) mayonnaise

1 tbsp (15 ml) apple cider vinegar

2 tbsp (30 ml) pickle juice

1 tbsp (15 g) prepared horseradish

1 tsp freshly squeezed lemon juice

½ tbsp (7 ml) Dijon mustard

½ tsp garlic powder

½ tsp onion powder

¼ tsp cayenne pepper

½ tbsp (7 g) brown sugar

Salt and pepper, to taste

FOR SERVING

Alabama White Sauce

2 tbsp (12 g) chopped green onion

Carrot and celery sticks

With a paper towel, pat the wings dry. In a small bowl, combine the smoked paprika, brown sugar, granulated sugar, chili powder, onion powder, garlic powder, chipotle powder, salt and pepper. Sprinkle the prepared rub over the wings, coating evenly.

Preheat the grill or smoker to 350°F (180°C), indirect heat.

Grill the wings for 40 minutes or until they reach a minimum internal temperature of 165°F (75°C), or 190°F (90°C) if you like them well done, flipping them halfway through the cooking time. To crisp the skin, move the wings to the direct heat side of the grill, turning occasionally, until the skin is dark golden or to your liking.

Meanwhile, prepare the sauce. In a medium bowl, whisk together the mayonnaise, apple cider vinegar, pickle juice, horseradish, lemon juice, Dijon mustard, garlic powder, onion powder, cayenne pepper, brown sugar, salt and pepper. Set aside.

Plate the wings and drizzle with the Alabama White Sauce. Garnish them with green onion and serve them with leftover sauce for dipping and carrot and celery sticks.

BIG GAME HOT

These are the BEST game day hot wings. However, you don't need to limit them to just game day, because they are perfect for any occasion. They are sweet, spicy and absolutely necessary to make. Pull this recipe out of your back pocket to please your guests. Cue "the crowd goes wild!" There will be a lot of high fives and cheers in the end. You're officially the MVP of the chicken wing game.

SERVINGS: 4

2 lb (907 g) chicken wings, tips removed, drums and flats separated

1 tsp garlic powder

1 tsp onion powder

1 tsp paprika

½ tsp cayenne pepper

1 tsp brown sugar

¼ tsp chili powder

Salt and pepper, to taste

BIG GAME SAUCE

½ cup (120 ml) Frank's RedHot Original

½ cup (120 ml) white vinegar

2 cups (480 ml) water

1 cup (192 g) granulated sugar

1 tsp crushed red pepper flakes

⅔ cup (160 ml) yellow mustard

3–4 tbsp (45–60 ml) ketchup

1 tsp garlic powder

Salt and pepper, to taste

FOR SERVING

2 tbsp (12 g) chopped green onion

Ranch or blue cheese dressing

Carrot and celery sticks

With a paper towel, pat the wings dry. In a small bowl, combine the garlic powder, onion powder, paprika, cayenne, brown sugar, chili powder, salt and pepper. Sprinkle the prepared rub over the wings, coating evenly.

Preheat the grill or smoker to 350°F (180°C), indirect heat.

Grill the wings for 40 minutes or until they reach a minimum internal temperature of 165°F (75°C), or 190°F (90°C) if you like them well done, flipping them halfway through the cooking time. To crisp the skin, move the wings to the direct heat side of the grill, turning occasionally, until the skin is dark golden or to your liking.

Meanwhile, prepare the sauce. In a medium saucepan over medium heat, whisk together the hot sauce, white vinegar, water, granulated sugar and crushed red pepper flakes. Bring to a boil, then whisk in the yellow mustard, ketchup, garlic powder, salt and pepper. Bring to a boil and reduce the heat to low. Simmer for 4 to 5 minutes or until the sauce has thickened to your liking.

Transfer the wings to a bowl and toss with Big Game Sauce until completely coated. Place them back on the grill grates for 5 to 10 minutes, until the sauce settles, or serve immediately.

Plate the wings and garnish them with green onion. Serve them with ranch or blue cheese dressing for dipping and carrot and celery sticks.

*See image on page 33 (shown on the left).

CHERRY COLA

These chicken wings are sticky, sweet, slightly spicy and perfect for any occasion. They are tossed in a lip-smacking Cherry Cola BBQ Sauce that's great as a dipping sauce. This sticky glaze will impress your friends and family. These wings will be on rotation once you try them. They're simple to make and irresistibly delicious.

SERVINGS: 4

2 lb (907 g) chicken wings, tips removed, drums and flats separated

1 tsp garlic powder

1 tsp onion powder

1 tsp paprika

2 tsp brown sugar

⅛ tsp cayenne pepper

¼ tsp chili powder

Salt and pepper, to taste

CHERRY COLA BBQ SAUCE

½ cup (120 ml) ketchup

¼ cup (60 ml) cherry juice

½ cup (120 ml) Coca-Cola®

1 tsp Sriracha hot sauce, or to taste

2 tbsp (28 g) brown sugar

1 tbsp (15 ml) low-sodium soy sauce

2 cloves garlic, minced

1 tsp smoked paprika

Salt and pepper, to taste

FOR SERVING

2 tbsp (12 g) chopped green onion

Leftover Cherry Cola BBQ Sauce

Ranch or blue cheese dressing

Carrot and celery sticks

With a paper towel, pat the wings dry. In a small bowl, combine the garlic powder, onion powder, paprika, brown sugar, cayenne, chili powder, salt and pepper. Sprinkle the prepared rub over the wings, coating evenly.

Preheat the grill or smoker to 350°F (180°C), indirect heat.

Grill the wings for 40 minutes or until they reach a minimum internal temperature of 165°F (75°C), or 190°F (90°C) if you like them well done, flipping them halfway through the cooking time. To crisp the skin, move the wings to the direct heat side of the grill, turning occasionally, until the skin is dark golden or to your liking.

Meanwhile, prepare the sauce. In a medium saucepan over medium heat, whisk together the ketchup, cherry juice, Coca-Cola, Sriracha, brown sugar, soy sauce, garlic, smoked paprika, salt and pepper. Bring to a boil, stirring frequently. Reduce the heat to low and simmer for 10 to 15 minutes until the sauce reduces and thickens, stirring occasionally.

Transfer the wings to a bowl and toss with Cherry Cola BBQ Sauce until completely coated.

Place the wings back on the grill grates for 5 to 10 minutes, until the sauce settles, or serve immediately. Plate the wings and garnish them with green onion. Serve them with leftover sauce and/or ranch or blue cheese dressing for dipping and carrot and celery sticks.

*See image on page 33 (shown on the right).

HOT STRIPE RANCH

If you're a lover of ranch dressing, you can have your wing and dip it too! These wings are seasoned in a ranch mixture, tossed in ranch dressing and finished off with a hot sauce drizzle. This combo will be your latest obsession! I've made these more times than I care to admit—they are one of my favorites. These are guaranteed to be a hit at any party, game day or as a weeknight meal.

SERVINGS: 4

2 lb (907 g) chicken wings, tips removed, drums and flats separated

½ tsp garlic powder

½ tsp onion powder

½ tsp paprika

⅛ tsp cayenne pepper

2 tbsp (28 g) ranch seasoning mix (I use Hidden Valley®)

Black pepper, to taste

Ranch dressing

FOR SERVING

Frank's RedHot Original or your favorite hot sauce

2 tbsp (12 g) chopped green onion

Blue cheese or ranch dressing

Carrot and celery sticks

With a paper towel, pat the wings dry. In a small bowl, combine the garlic powder, onion powder, paprika, cayenne, ranch seasoning and pepper. Sprinkle the prepared rub over the wings, coating evenly.

Preheat the grill or smoker to 350°F (180°C), indirect heat.

Grill the wings for 40 minutes or until they reach a minimum internal temperature of 165°F (75°C), or 190°F (90°C) if you like them well done, flipping them halfway through the cooking time. To crisp the skin, move the wings to the direct heat side of the grill, turning occasionally, until the skin is dark golden or to your liking.

Transfer the wings to a bowl and toss with ranch dressing until completely coated. Plate the wings and drizzle with hot sauce and garnish them with green onion. Serve them with blue cheese or ranch dressing for dipping and carrot and celery sticks.

HONEY GARLIC

These wings are sweet, sticky, garlicky and have a hint of caramel flavor. They are a classic that everyone will love, and they're the perfect mild option for anyone that is not a fan of spicy wings. There's something about this flavor combo that will have you coming back for more!

SERVINGS: 4

2 lb (907 g) chicken wings, tips removed, drums and flats separated

1 tsp garlic powder

1 tsp onion powder

1 tsp paprika

1/8 tsp cayenne pepper (optional)

1 tsp brown sugar

Salt and pepper, to taste

HONEY GARLIC SAUCE

1/2 cup (120 ml) low-sodium soy sauce

5 tbsp (75 ml) honey

2 tbsp (30 ml) water

1 tsp brown sugar

6 large cloves garlic, minced

1 tbsp (6 g) minced ginger

Salt and pepper, to taste

FOR SERVING

Sesame seeds

2 tbsp (12 g) chopped green onion

Leftover Honey Garlic Sauce

Ranch dressing (optional)

With a paper towel, pat the wings dry. In a small bowl, combine the garlic powder, onion powder, paprika, cayenne (if using), brown sugar, salt and pepper. Sprinkle the prepared rub over the wings, coating evenly.

Preheat the grill or smoker to 350°F (180°C), indirect heat.

Grill the wings for 40 minutes or until they reach a minimum internal temperature of 165°F (75°C), or 190°F (90°C) if you like them well done, flipping them halfway through the cooking time. To crisp the skin, move the wings to the direct heat side of the grill, turning occasionally, until the skin is dark golden or to your liking.

Meanwhile, prepare the sauce. In a large saucepan over medium heat, whisk together the soy sauce, honey, water, brown sugar, garlic, ginger, salt and pepper. Bring to a boil, stirring occasionally. Reduce heat to low and simmer for about 5 minutes or until the sauce reduces and thickens, stirring frequently.

Transfer the wings to a bowl and toss with Honey Garlic Sauce until completely coated. Plate the wings and garnish them with sesame seeds and green onion. Serve them with leftover sauce and/or ranch dressing for dipping.

STICKY TERIYAKI

These wings are sweet, savory and, of course, sticky. They are easy to make and perfect for busy weeknights or to serve a crowd. Make the sauce ahead of time and warm it up when you're ready to toss these incredibly delicious wings. Top them with sesame seeds and green onion for a finishing touch.

SERVINGS: 4

2 lb (907 g) chicken wings, tips removed, drums and flats separated
1 tsp garlic powder
1 tsp onion powder
1 tsp paprika
1 tsp brown sugar
½ tsp ginger powder
Salt and pepper, to taste
1 tbsp (15 ml) sesame oil

STICKY TERIYAKI SAUCE
½ cup (120 ml) low-sodium soy sauce
2–3 tbsp (30–45 ml) honey
2 tbsp (30 ml) water
½ tsp rice vinegar
½ tbsp (7 g) brown sugar
2 cloves garlic, minced
1 tsp minced ginger
¼ tsp black pepper

FOR SERVING
Sesame seeds
2 tbsp (12 g) chopped green onion
Leftover Sticky Teriyaki Sauce
Ranch dressing (optional)

With a paper towel, pat the wings dry. In a small bowl, combine the garlic powder, onion powder, paprika, brown sugar, ginger powder, salt and pepper. Toss the wings in sesame oil and sprinkle them with the prepared rub, coating evenly.

Preheat the grill or smoker to 350°F (180°C), indirect heat.

Grill the wings for 40 minutes or until they reach a minimum internal temperature of 165°F (75°C), or 190°F (90°C) if you like them well done, flipping them halfway through the cooking time. To crisp the skin, move the wings to the direct heat side of the grill, turning occasionally, until the skin is dark golden or to your liking.

Meanwhile, prepare the sauce. In a large saucepan over medium heat, whisk together the soy sauce, honey, water, rice vinegar, brown sugar, garlic, ginger and pepper. Bring to a boil, stirring occasionally. Reduce heat to low and simmer for about 5 minutes or until the sauce reduces and thickens, stirring frequently.

Transfer the wings to a bowl and toss with the Sticky Teriyaki Sauce until completely coated. Plate the wings and garnish them with sesame seeds and green onion. Serve them with leftover sauce and/or ranch dressing.

* See image on page 39 (shown on the left).

GRILL MASTER

These chicken wings will have your friends and family calling you grill master in no time. They are simple to prepare and full of flavor! They are marinated in a mouthwatering sauce that includes Italian-style dressing and cayenne pepper to make these wings tender, juicy, savory and slightly spicy. Your guests will be begging for more, so be sure to make extra.

SERVINGS: 4

2 lb (907 g) chicken wings, tips removed, drums and flats separated

½ cup (120 ml) Italian-style salad dressing

½ cup (120 ml) low-sodium soy sauce

¼ tsp paprika

¼ tsp brown sugar

⅛ tsp chili powder

¼ tsp onion powder

¼ tsp garlic powder

⅛ tsp cayenne pepper (optional)

GRILL MASTER SAUCE

¼ cup (56 g) unsalted butter

1 tsp minced garlic

1 tsp low-sodium soy sauce

¼ cup (60 ml) Frank's RedHot Original

FOR SERVING

2 tbsp (12 g) chopped green onion

Ranch or blue cheese dressing

Carrot and celery sticks

With a paper towel, pat the wings dry. Place the wings in a shallow dish or resealable plastic bag. In a medium bowl, whisk together the Italian dressing, soy sauce, paprika, brown sugar, chili powder, onion powder, garlic powder and cayenne (if using). Pour the marinade onto the wings, and toss to coat. Cover and refrigerate for a minimum of 4 hours or overnight (the longer the better for best flavor results).

Preheat the grill or smoker to 350°F (180°C), indirect heat.

Grill the wings for 40 minutes or until they reach a minimum internal temperature of 165°F (75°C), or 190°F (90°C) if you like them well done, flipping them halfway through the cooking time. To crisp the skin, move the wings to the direct heat side of the grill, turning occasionally, until the skin is dark golden or to your liking.

Meanwhile, prepare the sauce. In a small saucepan over medium heat, melt the butter with the garlic until fragrant, 2 to 3 minutes. Stir in the soy sauce and hot sauce. Simmer on low for 2 to 3 minutes.

Transfer the wings to a bowl and toss with the Grill Master Sauce until completely coated. Plate the wings and garnish with green onion. Serve them with ranch or blue cheese dressing for dipping and carrot and celery sticks.

* See image on page 39 (shown on the right).

MANGO HABAÑERO

Upgrade your next game day with this addictive recipe that will make your chicken wings stand out from the rest. The sauce is a beautiful, bright orange blend of mango, habañero peppers, spices, lime juice and honey. Coat the wings with cornstarch for a crispy finish! The result is a perfect balance of sweet and heat.

SERVINGS: 4

2 lb (907 g) chicken wings, tips removed, drums and flats separated

1 tsp paprika

¼ tsp chili powder

⅛ tsp cayenne pepper

1 tsp garlic powder

1 tsp onion powder

Salt and pepper, to taste

1 tsp cornstarch

MANGO HABAÑERO SAUCE

1 ripe mango, peeled and chopped

6 habañero peppers, chopped (use more or fewer, as desired)

3 cloves garlic, peeled

¼ cup (60 ml) apple cider vinegar

2 tbsp (30 ml) lime juice

¼ cup (60 ml) honey

FOR SERVING

Carrot and celery sticks

Leftover Mango Habañero Sauce

Ranch dressing (optional)

With a paper towel, pat the wings dry. In a small bowl, combine the paprika, chili powder, cayenne, garlic powder, onion powder, salt, pepper and cornstarch. Sprinkle the prepared rub over the wings, coating evenly.

Preheat the grill or smoker to 350°F (180°C), indirect heat.

Grill the wings for 40 minutes or until they reach a minimum internal temperature of 165°F (75°C), or 190°F (90°C) if you like them well done, flipping them halfway through the cooking time. To crisp the skin, move the wings to the direct heat side of the grill, turning occasionally, until the skin is dark golden or to your liking.

Meanwhile, prepare the sauce. In a food processor or blender, add the mango, habañero peppers, garlic, apple cider vinegar and lime juice. Blend until fully combined and smooth.

In a saucepan over medium-low heat, combine the honey with the mango habañero mixture. Stir frequently to prevent sticking and simmer for 5 to 10 minutes, or until the sauce reaches your preferred consistency.

Transfer the wings to a bowl and toss them with the Mango Habañero Sauce until completely coated. Place the wings back on the grill grate for 5 to 10 minutes, until the sauce settles, or serve immediately.

Serve them with carrot and celery sticks, leftover sauce and/or ranch dressing.

FRESH CHIMI-CHURRI

Chimichurri sauce is popular on steak, but it is a MUST try on chicken wings. It is simple to prepare with a handful of ingredients and once you make it, you'll always want some on hand. These wings are incredibly vibrant, packed with fresh flavor, crispy and juicy. The leftover sauce is perfect for dipping. Adjust the heat to your preference.

SERVINGS: 4

2 lb (907 g) chicken wings, tips removed, drums and flats separated

CHIMICHURRI MARINADE

½ cup (120 ml) extra-virgin olive oil

¼ cup (15 g) finely chopped flat-leaf parsley

½ cup (8 g) finely chopped cilantro

¼ cup (60 ml) red wine vinegar

¾ tsp dried oregano

3 cloves garlic, minced

1 finely chopped shallot or 2 tsp (5 g) finely chopped red onion

1 tsp finely chopped red chili, or to taste

1 tsp crushed red pepper flakes, or to taste

1 tsp paprika

1–2 tsp (5–10 ml) freshly squeezed lemon juice

Salt and pepper, to taste

FOR SERVING

Leftover Chimichurri Marinade

2 tbsp (2 g) chopped cilantro

Finely chopped red chili

Lime wedges

With a paper towel, pat the wings dry. Place the wings in a shallow dish or resealable plastic bag. In a large bowl, combine the olive oil, parsley, cilantro, red wine vinegar, oregano, garlic, shallot, red chili, crushed red pepper flakes, paprika, lemon juice, salt and pepper. Pour enough of the marinade to cover the wings and toss to coat. Reserve the rest for later, to top the chicken wings. Cover and refrigerate for a minimum of 2 hours or overnight (the longer the better for best flavor results).

Preheat the grill or smoker to 350°F (180°C), indirect heat.

Grill the wings for 40 minutes or until they reach a minimum internal temperature of 165°F (75°C), or 190°F (90°C) if you like them well done, flipping them halfway through the cooking time. To crisp the skin, move the wings to the direct heat side of the grill, turning occasionally, until the skin is dark golden or to your liking.

Plate the wings and garnish them with extra unused Chimichurri Marinade, cilantro and red chilies. Serve them with lime wedges.

CHIPOTLE HONEY

These chicken wings are sweet, smoky, spicy and perfect for entertaining a crowd or your family. Be warned: they're addictive. They pair perfectly with my delicious Avocado Crema Dipping Sauce for a slam dunk finish. Keep some napkins nearby—these are sticky.

SERVINGS: 4

2 lb (907 g) chicken wings, tips removed, drums and flats separated

½ cup (119 g) chipotle peppers in adobo sauce

¼ cup (60 ml) honey

¼ cup (60 ml) lime juice

1 tsp garlic powder

1 tsp onion powder

Salt and pepper, to taste

2 tbsp (15 g) your favorite BBQ rub

AVOCADO CREMA DIPPING SAUCE

1 large avocado, halved and pitted

¼ cup (60 ml) sour cream

1 tbsp (15 ml) lime juice

1 tbsp (15 ml) apple cider vinegar

¼ cup (4 g) cilantro

1–2 tbsp (15–30 ml) water

Salt and pepper, to taste

FOR SERVING

2 tbsp (12 g) chopped green onion

Avocado Crema Dipping Sauce

Carrot and celery sticks

With a paper towel, pat the wings dry. Place the wings in a shallow dish or resealable plastic bag. Place the chipotle peppers in adobo sauce, honey, lime juice, garlic powder, onion powder, salt and pepper in a food processor or blender. Blend until smooth. Pour the marinade onto the wings and toss to coat. Keep any excess marinade aside to baste the wings. Cover and refrigerate for a minimum of 4 hours or overnight (the longer the better for best flavor results).

With a paper towel, pat the wings dry. Sprinkle your favorite rub over the wings, coating evenly.

Preheat the grill or smoker to 350°F (180°C), indirect heat.

Grill the wings for 40 minutes or until they reach a minimum internal temperature of 165°F (75°C), or 190°F (90°C) if you like them well done, flipping them halfway through the cooking time. To crisp the skin, move the wings to the direct heat side of the grill, turning occasionally, until the skin is dark golden or to your liking. Baste the wings with the reserved marinade in the last 5 minutes.

Meanwhile, prepare the dipping sauce. Place the avocado, sour cream, lime juice, apple cider vinegar, cilantro, water, salt and pepper into a blender. Blend until smooth.

Plate the wings and garnish with the green onion. Serve them with the Avocado Crema Dipping Sauce and carrot and celery sticks.

SALT AND VINEGAR

Chips are my favorite snack—once I start, it's hard to stop. Facts. If you love salt and vinegar chips, then these wings are screaming your name! Even if you've never tried the chip flavor, you must make these. They are tangy, salty and will have you hooked after just one bite—you won't be able to resist! They're perfect for game day or any day.

SERVINGS: 4

2 lb (907 g) chicken wings, tips removed, drums and flats separated

SALT AND VINEGAR MARINADE

½ cup (120 ml) white vinegar

6 tbsp (90 ml) malt vinegar or apple cider vinegar

2 tbsp (36 g) flaky sea salt

2¼ tsp (11 g) ranch seasoning mix (I use Hidden Valley)

1 tsp brown sugar

½ tsp garlic powder

¼ tsp onion powder

FOR SERVING

2 tbsp (12 g) chopped green onion

Flaky sea salt (optional)

Ranch or blue cheese dressing

Carrot and celery sticks

With a paper towel, pat the wings dry. Place the wings in a shallow dish or resealable plastic bag. In a medium bowl, whisk to combine the white vinegar, malt vinegar, sea salt, ranch seasoning, brown sugar, garlic powder and onion powder. Pour half of the marinade over the wings. Toss to coat. Cover and refrigerate for 3 hours or overnight (the longer the better for best flavor results). Shake any excess off and discard the marinade.

Preheat the grill or smoker to 350°F (180°C), indirect heat.

Grill the wings for 40 minutes or until they reach a minimum internal temperature of 165°F (75°C), or 190°F (90°C) if you like them well done, flipping them halfway through the cooking time.

Turn the grill up to 400°F (200°C). Transfer the wings to a bowl and toss with the remaining Salt and Vinegar Marinade. Place them back on the grill grates to crisp the skin, turning occasionally until the skin is dark golden or to your liking.

Plate the wings and garnish them with green onion and sea salt (if using). Serve them with ranch or blue cheese dressing for dipping and carrot and celery sticks.

*See image on page 46 (shown on the top).

HONEY BUFFALO

These Honey Buffalo chicken wings have the perfect balance of sweet and heat! You won't be able to take your eyes off of the glossy sauce the honey creates. These wings are crispy, saucy and perfect for any occasion including a weeknight meal or appetizer. Serve them with plenty of napkins.

SERVINGS: 4

2 lb (907 g) chicken wings, tips removed, drums and flats separated

1 tsp garlic powder

1 tsp onion powder

1 tsp smoked paprika

1/4 tsp chili powder

1/8 tsp cayenne pepper

1 tsp brown sugar

Salt and pepper, to taste

1 tsp cornstarch

HONEY BUFFALO SAUCE

1/2 cup (120 ml) Frank's RedHot Original

5 tbsp (75 ml) honey

1 tsp garlic powder

1/4 tsp black pepper

4 tbsp (56 g) unsalted butter

FOR SERVING

Ranch or blue cheese dressing

Carrot and celery sticks

With a paper towel, pat the wings dry. In a small bowl, combine the garlic powder, onion powder, smoked paprika, chili powder, cayenne, brown sugar, salt, pepper and cornstarch. Sprinkle the prepared rub over the wings, coating evenly.

Preheat the grill or smoker to 350°F (180°C), indirect heat.

Grill the wings for 40 minutes or until they reach a minimum internal temperature of 165°F (75°C), or 190°F (90°C) if you like them well done, flipping them halfway through the cooking time. To crisp the skin, move the wings to the direct heat side of the grill, turning occasionally, until the skin is dark golden or to your liking.

Meanwhile, prepare the sauce. In a small saucepan over medium-low heat, whisk together the hot sauce, honey, garlic powder and pepper. Bring to a simmer, then stir in the butter. Cook until the butter is melted and slightly reduced, about 2 minutes.

Transfer the wings to a bowl and toss with the Honey Buffalo Sauce until completely coated. Plate the wings and serve them with ranch or blue cheese dressing for dipping and carrot and celery sticks.

*See image on page 46 (shown on the left).

OLD BAY® BAE

Old Bay seasoning is a classic dating back to 1939 and is mostly used in seafood dishes, but it's so versatile that it can be used on anything! In come Old Bay Bae chicken wings tossed in a lemon butter sauce that will make your taste buds dance. They are smoky, spicy, salty and peppery. Perfectly paired with an ice-cold beer, you'll be pleasantly surprised by how incredibly delicious this combo is.

SERVINGS: 4

2 lb (907 g) chicken wings, tips removed, drums and flats separated

¼ tsp garlic powder

¼ tsp onion powder

4 tbsp (56 g) unsalted butter

1–2 lemon wedges

OLD BAY–STYLE SEASONING

¾ tbsp (11 g) salt, or to taste (see Note)

¼ tsp cayenne pepper

1 tbsp (14 g) celery salt (see Note)

1 tsp ground celery seeds

2 tsp (6 g) sweet paprika

½ tsp smoked paprika

1 tsp ground dry mustard

1 tsp ground ginger

2 tsp (6 g) ground bay leaves

½ tsp black pepper

½ tsp white pepper

⅛ tsp ground nutmeg

⅛ tsp ground mace

⅛ tsp ground cardamom

⅛ tsp ground allspice

⅛ tsp ground cinnamon

1/16 tsp ground cloves

FOR SERVING

2 tbsp (8 g) chopped parsley

Ranch dressing

Carrot and celery sticks

With a paper towel, pat the wings dry. Make the seasoning. In a medium bowl, combine the salt, cayenne, celery salt, ground celery seeds, sweet paprika, smoked paprika, ground dry mustard, ground ginger, ground bay leaves, black pepper, white pepper, nutmeg, mace, cardamom, allspice, cinnamon and cloves. Sprinkle the garlic powder, onion powder and prepared Old Bay–Style Seasoning over the wings, coating evenly. Store leftover seasoning in an airtight container.

Preheat the grill or smoker to 350°F (180°C), indirect heat.

Grill the wings for 40 minutes or until they reach a minimum internal temperature of 165°F (75°C), or 190°F (90°C) if you like them well done, flipping them halfway through the cooking time. To crisp the skin, move the wings to the direct heat side of the grill, turning occasionally, until the skin is dark golden or to your liking.

In a small saucepan over medium heat, melt the butter. Transfer the wings to a bowl, pour on the melted butter and squeeze 1 to 2 lemon wedges over the top. Toss to coat. Plate the wings and garnish them with the parsley. Serve them with ranch dressing and carrot and celery sticks.

NOTE: Depending on your salt intake preference, do not add the ¾ tablespoon (11 g) of salt at first. Taste the combined seasoning without it, then add if necessary. You can also start with half the amount of celery salt.

COMFORT FOOD FAVORITES

Comfort food in the form of chicken wings—does it get any better? There are days when you're just craving something more comforting than your sweatpants to soothe your soul. This chapter has everything: pizza, nachos, tacos, pasta and much more. Some of my favorites include Chili Cheese (page 60), Smoke 'n' Fried (page 61), Big Dill (page 64) and Birria Style (page 74). You'll be blown away by these incredibly delicious combos. They are perfect for any occasion. Go ahead and indulge!

NACHO SUPREME

Loaded nachos are ALWAYS a good idea, especially when they're paired with chicken wings and a cold beer. These Nacho Supreme wings have it all: beer cheese, diced tomatoes, jalapeños and all your favorite fixings. Combining two favorite bar comfort foods to give you a flavor experience like no other, this recipe will quickly become your go-to!

SERVINGS: 4

2 lb (907 g) chicken wings, tips removed, drums and flats separated

1 tbsp (8 g) paprika

1 tbsp (14 g) brown sugar

1 tsp cayenne pepper

1 tsp chili powder

½ tsp cumin

1 tsp onion powder

1 tsp garlic powder

Salt and pepper, to taste

BEER CHEESE SAUCE

8 oz (240 g) cream cheese, softened to room temperature and cubed

1 cup (240 ml) beer

1 (1 oz [28-g]) packet ranch salad dressing mix

2 cups (210 g) shredded cheddar cheese

FOR SERVING

2 tbsp (25 g) diced tomato

½ tbsp (4 g) diced red onion

1 tbsp (6 g) chopped green onion

1 tsp chopped cilantro

Jalapeño slices (optional)

Salsa

Sour cream

Guacamole

Beer Cheese Sauce

With a paper towel, pat the wings dry. In a small bowl, combine the paprika, brown sugar, cayenne, chili powder, cumin, onion powder, garlic powder, salt and pepper. Sprinkle the prepared rub over the wings, coating evenly.

Preheat the grill or smoker to 350°F (180°C), indirect heat.

Grill the wings for 40 minutes or until they reach a minimum internal temperature of 165°F (75°C), or 190°F (90°C) if you like them well done, flipping them halfway through the cooking time. To crisp the skin, move the wings to the direct heat side of the grill, turning occasionally, until the skin is dark golden or to your liking.

Meanwhile, prepare the sauce. In a small pot over medium heat, add the cubed cream cheese and melt, about 5 minutes. Add the beer, slowly stirring until fully combined with the cream cheese. Add the ranch salad dressing mix and stir. Remove from the heat and add the cheddar cheese little by little, stirring continuously until all the cheese is fully melted.

Plate the wings and drizzle with as much Beer Cheese Sauce as desired. Top with the tomato, onion, green onion, cilantro and jalapeño slices, if using. Serve them with salsa, sour cream, guacamole and more Beer Cheese Sauce.

TACO TUESDAY

Taco Tuesday is all the rave on social media, and why wouldn't it be? I love tacos on Tuesday, or any day for that matter, and chicken wings on Wednesday for Wing Crush Wednesday (WCW), so naturally I would make a 2 for 1. Say hello to Taco Tuesday chicken wings! Topped with Pico de Gallo, they are all the flavors you love on tacos in the form of wings. My taco rub has the perfect balance of flavor and heat, while my Pico de Gallo adds the finishing touch. Grab a *cerveza* and enjoy!

SERVINGS: 4

2 lb (907 g) chicken wings, tips removed, drums and flats separated

2 tsp (6 g) chili powder

½ tsp ground cumin

½ tsp garlic powder

½ tsp onion powder

½ tsp paprika

¼ tsp oregano

¼ tsp cayenne pepper

1 tsp cornstarch

Salt and pepper, to taste

PICO DE GALLO

½ cup (80 g) finely chopped onion

½ finely chopped jalapeño

2 tbsp (30 ml) freshly squeezed lime juice

Salt, to taste

2 tomatoes, chopped

¼ cup (4 g) chopped cilantro

FOR SERVING

Chopped cilantro

Ranch dressing

With a paper towel, pat the wings dry. In a small bowl, combine the chili powder, cumin, garlic powder, onion powder, paprika, oregano, cayenne, cornstarch, salt and pepper. Sprinkle the prepared rub over the wings, coating evenly.

Meanwhile prepare the Pico de Gallo. In a medium bowl, combine the chopped onion, jalapeño, lime juice and salt. Set aside for about 5 minutes. Add the chopped tomatoes and cilantro, and stir to combine. Taste and add more salt, if necessary. Cover and refrigerate until ready to serve.

Preheat the grill or smoker to 350°F (180°C), indirect heat.

Grill the wings for 40 minutes or until they reach a minimum internal temperature of 165°F (75°C), or 190°F (90°C) if you like them well done, flipping them halfway through the cooking time. To crisp the skin, move the wings to the direct heat side of the grill, turning occasionally, until the skin is dark golden or to your liking.

Plate the wings and garnish them with as much Pico de Gallo and cilantro as you like. Serve them with ranch dressing for dipping. Don't forget the tortilla chips to finish off any leftover Pico de Gallo.

PEPPERONI PIZZA

These wings are the ULTIMATE mash-up of my two favorite game day foods. I don't know about you, but in my house whenever there is a sporting event or even just a Friday night, pizza and wings are always on the table. Melted cheese and crispy pepperoni paired with my Creamy Garlic Dipping Sauce are a dream come true. Grab a beer, sit back and enjoy!

SERVINGS: 4

2 lb (907 g) chicken wings, tip removed, drums and flats separated

1 tsp garlic powder

1 tsp onion powder

1 tsp oregano

1 tsp Italian seasoning

Salt and pepper, to taste

1 cup (240 ml) pizza sauce

¾ cup (84 g) shredded mozzarella cheese

½ cup (67 g) pepperoni minis (I use Hormel®) or regular-sized pepperoni sliced into smaller pieces

CREAMY GARLIC DIPPING SAUCE

½ cup (120 ml) Caesar dressing

2 tbsp (15 g) grated Parmesan cheese

¼ cup (60 ml) mayonnaise

4 cloves garlic, minced

1 tsp parsley flakes

¼ tsp black pepper

FOR SERVING

Crushed red pepper flakes

Grated Parmesan cheese

Dried oregano

Creamy Garlic Dipping Sauce

With a paper towel, pat the wings dry. Place the wings in a shallow dish or resealable plastic bag. In a small bowl, combine the garlic powder, onion powder, oregano, Italian seasoning, salt and pepper. Sprinkle the prepared rub over the wings, coating evenly. Pour about ¾ cup (180 ml) of pizza sauce over the wings and toss to coat evenly. Set the rest aside for later. Cover and refrigerate for 2 to 6 hours (the longer the better for best flavor results).

Prepare the dipping sauce. In a medium bowl, combine the Caesar dressing, Parmesan cheese, mayonnaise, garlic, parsley flakes and pepper. Cover and refrigerate until ready to serve.

Preheat the grill or smoker to 350°F (180°C), indirect heat.

Grill the wings for 40 minutes or until they reach a minimum internal temperature of 165°F (75°C), or 190°F (90°C) if you like them well done, flipping them halfway through the cooking time. To crisp the skin, move the wings to the direct heat side of the grill, turning occasionally, until the skin is dark golden or to your liking. Baste the wings with the remaining pizza sauce in the last 5 minutes.

Turn the grill up to 400°F (204°C). Place the wings on a lined baking tray or cast-iron skillet. Top with the mozzarella cheese and pepperoni. Place back on the grill for 5 to 10 minutes or until the cheese has melted to your liking.

Plate the wings and garnish them with crushed red pepper flakes, Parmesan cheese and oregano. Serve them with Creamy Garlic Dipping Sauce.

CHILI CHEESE

Do you have some leftover chili you need to use up? Perfect, let's make wings! Even if you don't have leftovers, you're going to want to make chili just for these Chili Cheese chicken wings. They are packed with classic chili flavors and drizzled with a simple and quick Salsa con Queso Sauce. These are the perfect comfort food to earn you a place in the Backyard BBQ Hall of Fame!

SERVINGS: 4

2 lb (907 g) chicken wings, tip removed, drums and flats separated

1 tsp garlic powder

1 tsp onion powder

1 tsp paprika

1 tsp brown sugar

½ tsp chili powder

¼ tsp ground cumin

¼ tsp cayenne pepper

Salt and pepper, to taste

¾ cup (180 g) leftover chili or canned chili such as Stagg® chili

Tortilla chips (I use Tostitos®)

SALSA CON QUESO SAUCE

½ cup (130 g) salsa (I use Tostitos medium salsa)

1½ cups (170 g) shredded cheddar cheese

4 oz (120 g) cream cheese, cut into cubes

¼ cup (60 ml) milk

Salt and pepper, to taste

FOR SERVING

1 tbsp (7 g) chopped red onion

½ jalapeño, sliced

2 tbsp (12 g) chopped green onion

Sour cream

With a paper towel, pat the wings dry. In a small bowl, combine the garlic powder, onion powder, paprika, brown sugar, chili powder, ground cumin, cayenne, salt and pepper. Sprinkle the prepared rub over the wings, coating evenly.

Preheat the grill or smoker to 350°F (180°C), indirect heat.

Grill the wings for 40 minutes or until they reach a minimum internal temperature of 165°F (75°C), or 190°F (90°C) if you like them well done, flipping them halfway through the cooking time. To crisp the skin, move the wings to the direct heat side of the grill, turning occasionally, until the skin is dark golden or to your liking.

Meanwhile, prepare the sauce. In a large saucepan over medium heat, combine the salsa, cheddar cheese, cream cheese, milk, salt and pepper. Stir frequently and bring to a boil. Reduce the heat and simmer for 2 minutes. Keep warm.

In a separate small saucepan, heat up the leftover chili or canned chili. Place the tortilla chips on a plate (enough to cover so you can scoop up any leftovers). Top with the wings, warm chili, Salsa con Queso Sauce, red onion, jalapeño slices and green onion. Serve with sour cream.

* See image on page 59 (shown on the right).

SMOKE 'N' FRIED

Do you like fried chicken wings? Do you also like smoked chicken wings? Why not have the best of both worlds with these Smoke 'n' Fried wings! They're smoked low and slow, then fried in hot oil for a crispy, crunchy finish and a slam dunk in my Chipotle-Ranch Dipping Sauce. Fried chicken is one of the quintessential comfort foods, so this recipe is the ultimate way to cook wings! Serve them dry rubbed or toss them in your favorite sauce. Your family and friends will be impressed.

SERVINGS: 4

2 lb (907 g) chicken wings, tips removed, drums and flats separated

1 tsp smoked paprika

2 tsp (10 g) brown sugar

1/4 tsp chili powder

1 tsp onion powder

1 tsp garlic powder

1/8 tsp cayenne pepper

Salt and pepper, to taste

Your favorite sauce to toss the wings (optional)

Vegetable oil, for frying

CHIPOTLE-RANCH DIPPING SAUCE

1/4 cup (60 ml) ranch dressing

2 tbsp (30 ml) mayonnaise

2 tbsp (30 ml) sour cream

1–2 tbsp (15–30 g) adobo sauce (from canned chipotle peppers)

1 tsp freshly squeezed lime juice

Salt and pepper, to taste

FOR SERVING

2 tbsp (12 g) chopped green onion

Chipotle-Ranch Dipping Sauce

Carrot and celery sticks

With a paper towel, pat the wings dry. In a small bowl, combine the smoked paprika, brown sugar, chili powder, onion powder, garlic powder, cayenne, salt and pepper. Sprinkle the prepared rub over the wings, coating evenly.

Preheat the grill or smoker to 225°F (110°C), indirect heat.

Smoke the wings for 1 to 1½ hours or until they reach a minimum internal temperature of 145°F (65°C), flipping them halfway through the cooking time.

Prepare the dipping sauce. In a medium bowl, whisk together the ranch dressing, mayonnaise, sour cream, adobo sauce, lime juice, salt and pepper. Set aside.

Meanwhile, preheat enough vegetable oil to cover the wings over medium-high heat in a cast-iron skillet, until the oil temperature is 375°F (191°C), or use a deep fryer. Fry the wings in batches making sure they don't overlap. Fry for 2 to 3 minutes, until the wings are a deep, golden crisp color or until they reach an internal temperature of 180°F (80°C).

If you're using a sauce, transfer the wings to a bowl and toss them with your favorite sauce until completely coated, or sprinkle with some of the remaining rub, toss to coat and plate the wings. Garnish them with green onion and serve them with the Chipotle-Ranch Dipping Sauce and carrot and celery sticks.

* See image on page 59 (shown on the left).

SPICY DELUXE

The spice is right and I'm addicted! These chicken wings are marinated in a blend of peppers and pickle juice to make them tender, juicy and oh so delicious! The compliments will be never-ending once you serve these at your next party, game day or backyard BBQ. These wings have the familiar flavors of a Chick-Fil-A® spicy deluxe chicken sandwich. Serve them with my Cilantro-Lime Dipping Sauce for a cool finish. Adjust the heat to your preference.

SERVINGS: 4

2 lb (907 g) chicken wings, tips removed, drums and flats separated

¼ cup (60 ml) dill pickle juice

¼ cup (60 ml) Frank's RedHot Original

1 tsp smoked paprika

2 tsp (10 g) brown sugar

1 tsp chili powder

1 tsp onion powder

1 tsp garlic powder

1–3 tsp (3–5 g) cayenne pepper, to taste

¼ tsp crushed red pepper flakes, or to taste

Salt and pepper, to taste

CILANTRO-LIME DIPPING SAUCE

¼ cup (60 ml) mayonnaise

¼ cup (60 ml) sour cream

½ avocado, peeled and pitted

1 clove garlic, minced

2 tbsp (2 g) chopped cilantro

Juice of 1 lime

1 tbsp (15 ml) extra-virgin olive oil

Salt and pepper, to taste

FOR SERVING

2 tbsp (12 g) chopped green onion

Cilantro-Lime Dipping Sauce

Carrot and celery sticks

With a paper towel, pat the wings dry. Place the wings in a shallow dish or resealable plastic bag. In a small bowl, combine the dill pickle juice, hot sauce, smoked paprika, brown sugar, chili powder, onion powder, garlic powder, cayenne, crushed red pepper flakes, salt and pepper. Pour in enough marinade to cover the wings. Keep any excess aside to baste the wings. Toss to coat. Cover and refrigerate for 4 hours or overnight, which I highly recommend (the longer the better for best flavor results). Shake any excess off and discard the marinade.

Preheat the grill or smoker to 350°F (180°C), indirect heat.

Grill the wings for 40 minutes or until they reach a minimum internal temperature of 165°F (75°C), or 190°F (90°C) if you like them well done, flipping them halfway through the cooking time. To crisp the skin, move the wings to the direct heat side of the grill, turning occasionally, until the skin is dark golden or to your liking. Baste the wings with the reserved marinade sauce in the last 5 to 10 minutes.

Meanwhile, prepare the dipping sauce. In a medium bowl, combine the mayonnaise, sour cream, avocado, garlic, cilantro, lime juice, olive oil, salt and pepper. Cover and refrigerate until ready to serve.

Plate the wings and garnish them with green onion. Serve them with Cilantro-Lime Dipping Sauce and carrot and celery sticks.

BIG DILL

Here's the dill, these chicken wings are brined in pickle juice to make them tender and juicy with a crispy finish. They are seasoned and tossed in a Garlic-Dill Butter Sauce for lip-smacking results! These will be your new obsession, as they are at our annual family picnic. If you love garlic pickles (like I do), then you need to make these. So, don't toss out that pickle juice next time you have an empty jar!

SERVINGS: 4

2 lb (907 g) chicken wings, tips removed, drums and flats separated

2 cups (480 ml) dill pickle juice or enough to cover wings

1 tsp dry dill

1 tsp garlic powder

1 tsp onion powder

1 tsp paprika

¼ tsp cayenne pepper (optional)

½ tsp ground mustard

Salt and pepper, to taste

DILL PICKLE DIPPING SAUCE

½ cup (120 ml) mayonnaise

½ cup (120 ml) sour cream

2 tbsp (7 g) finely chopped fresh dill

1 medium dill pickle, chopped

2 tbsp (30 ml) pickle juice

2 cloves garlic, minced

1 tsp freshly squeezed lemon juice

Salt and pepper, to taste

GARLIC-DILL BUTTER SAUCE

2 tbsp (28 g) unsalted butter

½ tsp finely chopped fresh dill

½ tsp minced garlic

¼ tsp black pepper

FOR SERVING

Dill Pickle Dipping Sauce

Carrot and celery sticks

With a paper towel, pat the wings dry. Place the wings in a shallow dish or resealable plastic bag and pour over enough pickle juice to cover the wings. Cover and refrigerate for 3 to 6 hours or overnight, if time permits (the longer the better).

Prepare the dipping sauce. In a medium bowl, combine the mayonnaise, sour cream, dill, dill pickle, pickle juice, garlic, lemon juice, salt and pepper. Cover and refrigerate until ready to serve.

In a small bowl, combine the dry dill, garlic powder, onion powder, paprika, cayenne (if using), ground mustard, salt and pepper. Remove the wings from the marinade and with a paper towel, pat them dry. Discard the marinade. Sprinkle the prepared rub over the wings, coating evenly.

Preheat the grill or smoker to 350°F (180°C), indirect heat.

Grill the wings for 40 minutes or until they reach a minimum internal temperature of 165°F (75°C), or 190°F (90°C) if you like them well done, flipping them halfway through the cooking time. To crisp the skin, move the wings to the direct heat side of the grill, turning occasionally, until the skin is dark golden or to your liking.

Transfer the wings to a bowl and top with the butter, fresh dill, garlic and pepper. Toss until completely coated. Plate the wings and serve them with the Dill Pickle Dipping Sauce and carrot and celery sticks.

GARLIC ALFREDO

These chicken wings will be a crowd favorite! They are tossed in a creamy, buttery, cheesy and garlicky Alfredo sauce that will have you drizzling more sauce over them like it's nobody's business. In true pasta house restaurant fashion, garnish them with more Parmesan cheese and cracked black pepper with a side of crushed red pepper flakes for added heat.

SERVINGS: 4

2 lb (907 g) chicken wings, tips removed, drums and flats separated

1 tsp garlic powder

1 tsp onion powder

1 tsp paprika

½ tsp Italian seasoning

¼ tsp cayenne pepper

Salt and pepper, to taste

1 tsp cornstarch

GARLIC ALFREDO SAUCE

4 tbsp (56 g) unsalted butter

2 tbsp (17 g) minced garlic

1 cup (240 ml) heavy cream

1¼ cups (125 g) grated Parmesan cheese

½ tsp black pepper

Salt, to taste

FOR SERVING

1 tbsp (7 g) grated Parmesan cheese (optional)

2 tbsp (8 g) chopped parsley

Leftover Garlic Alfredo Sauce

Carrot and celery sticks

With a paper towel, pat the wings dry. In a small bowl, combine the garlic powder, onion powder, paprika, Italian seasoning, cayenne, salt, pepper and cornstarch. Sprinkle the prepared rub over the wings, coating evenly.

Preheat the grill or smoker to 350°F (180°C), indirect heat.

Grill the wings for 40 minutes or until they reach a minimum internal temperature of 165°F (75°C), or 190°F (90°C) if you like them well done, flipping them halfway through the cooking time. To crisp the skin, move the wings to the direct heat side of the grill, turning occasionally, until the skin is dark golden or to your liking.

Meanwhile, prepare the sauce. In a large saucepan over medium heat, melt the butter. Add the garlic and sauté for 1 to 2 minutes, until fragrant. Next, add the heavy cream, Parmesan cheese, black pepper and salt. Stir until well blended.

Transfer the wings to a bowl and toss with the Garlic Alfredo Sauce until completely coated. Plate the wings and garnish them with Parmesan, if desired, and parsley. Serve them with the leftover sauce for dipping and celery and carrot sticks.

*See image on page 65 (shown on the top).

CAJUN BAY BAE

What do you get when you season your chicken wings with Cajun spices and toss them in my version of Old Bay hot sauce? The BEST EVER combo! Each of the two seasonings are used in some of my favorite comfort foods to serve when family and friends are over, so I decided to combine them and make one of my most requested wings. This combo is like no other and go together like Bey and Jay (if you know, you know).

SERVINGS: 4

2 lb (907 g) chicken wings, tips removed, drums and flats separated
1½ tbsp (10 g) paprika
1 tbsp (8 g) garlic powder
½ tbsp (4 g) onion powder
½ tbsp (3 g) cayenne pepper
¼ tsp red pepper flakes
1 tsp dried thyme
1 tsp dried oregano
½ tbsp (4 g) chili powder
½ tbsp (3 g) black pepper
½ tsp white pepper
½ tsp kosher salt, or to taste

BAY BAE HOT SAUCE
1 cup (240 ml) vinegar-based hot sauce (I use Frank's RedHot Original)
¼ cup (30 g) Old Bay seasoning (or use my recipe on page 50)
¼ cup (60 ml) water, to dilute if too salty

FOR SERVING
2 tbsp (12 g) chopped green onion
Ranch or Caesar dressing
Carrot and celery sticks

With a paper towel, pat the wings dry. In a small bowl, combine the paprika, garlic powder, onion powder, cayenne, red pepper flakes, thyme, oregano, chili powder, black pepper, white pepper and salt. Sprinkle some of the prepared rub over the wings, coating evenly. In a medium bowl, combine the hot sauce, Old Bay seasoning and water (if using). Set aside.

Preheat the grill or smoker to 350°F (180°C), indirect heat.

Grill the wings for 40 minutes or until they reach a minimum internal temperature of 165°F (75°C), or 190°F (90°C) if you like them well done, flipping them halfway through the cooking time. To crisp the skin, move the wings to the direct heat side of the grill, turning occasionally, until the skin is dark golden or to your liking.

Transfer the wings to a bowl, pour the Bay Bae Hot Sauce over them and toss until completely coated. Place them back on the grill grates for 5 to 10 minutes, until the sauce settles, or serve immediately. Plate the wings and garnish them with green onion. Serve them with ranch or Caesar dressing and carrot and celery sticks.

*See image on page 65 (shown on the left).

BACON JAM

Bacon makes everything better and these chicken wings are my jam. They're bursting with unforgettable flavors in a sweet and slightly spicy bacon jam sauce. This mouthwatering recipe will shake up your taste buds. You'll want to serve these at your next tailgate party.

SERVINGS: 4

BACON JAM SAUCE

1 lb (454 g) thin-cut bacon, chopped into small pieces

1 small yellow onion, finely diced

3 shallots, finely chopped

½ cup (110 g) brown sugar

½ cup (120 ml) maple syrup

½ cup (120 ml) apple cider vinegar

¼–½ tsp crushed red pepper flakes

½ cup (120 ml) freshly brewed coffee

1 tsp balsamic vinegar

½ cup (120 ml) water

2 lb (907 g) chicken wings, tips removed, drums and flats separated

Your favorite BBQ rub (I use Christie Vanover's Chicken Rub by Spiceology®)

FOR SERVING

2 tbsp (12 g) chopped green onion

Ranch or blue cheese dressing

Carrot and celery sticks

Prepare the sauce. In a large skillet over medium heat, cook the bacon until it starts to crisp, stirring frequently, about 10 minutes. Remove the bacon with a slotted spoon and drain it on a paper towel–lined plate. Reduce the heat to medium-low. Drain all but 1 tablespoon (15 ml) of bacon fat from the skillet, and add the onion and shallots. Cook until the onion caramelizes, about 20 minutes, stirring frequently. Add a splash of water if the skillet starts to get too dry. Next, return the bacon to the skillet and add the brown sugar, maple syrup, apple cider vinegar, red pepper flakes, coffee and balsamic vinegar. Increase the heat to medium-high and bring to a boil. Reduce the heat to low and cook for about 30 minutes or until the mixture has thickened to your liking, stirring occasionally. Add water if the mixture is too thick. Make sure to serve warm; reheat if needed.

With a paper towel, pat the wings dry. Sprinkle your favorite rub over the wings, coating evenly.

Preheat the grill or smoker to 350°F (180°C), indirect heat.

Grill the wings for 40 minutes or until they reach a minimum internal temperature of 165°F (75°C), or 190°F (90°C) if you like them well done, flipping them halfway through the cooking time. To crisp the skin, move the wings to the direct heat side of the grill, turning occasionally, until the skin is dark golden or to your liking.

Transfer the wings to a bowl and toss with the Bacon Jam Sauce until completely coated. Plate the wings and garnish them with green onion. Serve them with ranch or blue cheese dressing and carrot and celery sticks.

FLAMIN' BUFFALO

All I can think of while taking a bite out of these wings is … hot grill summer while "Fire Burning" by Sean Kingston plays in the background. These chicken wings are like no other, spicy yet full of flavor, and they taste like you're biting into Flamin' Hot Cheetos. They are brined in pickle juice and hot sauce to make them tender and juicy with a crispy finish. If you like spicy food, I HIGHLY recommend making these. You'll thank me later.

SERVINGS: 4

2 lb (907 g) chicken wings, tips removed, drums and flats separated

FLAMIN' BUFFALO MARINADE

¼ cup (60 ml) dill pickle juice

¼ cup (60 ml) Frank's RedHot Original

1 tsp smoked paprika

2 tsp (10 g) brown sugar

1 tsp chili powder

1 tsp onion powder

1 tsp garlic powder

1–3 tsp (3–5 g) cayenne pepper, or to taste

¼ tsp crushed red pepper flakes, or to taste

Salt and pepper, to taste

FLAMIN' BUFFALO DRY RUB

1 tsp smoked paprika

1 tsp brown sugar

½ tsp garlic powder

1 tsp onion powder

½ tsp cayenne pepper

1 tsp chipotle powder

1 tsp tomato soup mix powder (I use Knorr®)

Salt and pepper, to taste

FOR SERVING

2 tbsp (12 g) chopped green onion

Ranch or blue cheese dressing

Carrot and celery sticks

With a paper towel, pat the wings dry. Place the wings in a shallow dish or resealable plastic bag. Make the marinade. In a small bowl, combine the dill pickle juice, hot sauce, smoked paprika, brown sugar, chili powder, onion powder, garlic powder, cayenne, crushed red pepper flakes, salt and pepper. Pour enough marinade over the wings to cover them. Toss to coat. Cover and refrigerate for 4 hours or overnight (the longer the better for best flavor results).

Make the dry rub. In a small bowl, combine the smoked paprika, brown sugar, garlic powder, onion powder, cayenne, chipotle powder, tomato soup mix, salt and pepper. Remove the wings from the marinade and with a paper towel, pat them dry. Discard the marinade. Sprinkle the prepared rub over the wings, coating evenly.

Preheat the grill or smoker to 350°F (180°C), indirect heat.

Grill the wings for 40 minutes or until they reach a minimum internal temperature of 165°F (75°C), or 190°F (90°C) if you like them well done, flipping them halfway through the cooking time. To crisp the skin, move the wings to the direct heat side of the grill, turning occasionally, until the skin is dark golden or to your liking.

Plate the wings and garnish them with green onion. Serve them with ranch or blue cheese dressing for dipping and carrot and celery sticks.

CHICKEN PARMESAN

The great debate! Is it Chicken Parmesan or Chicken Parmigiana? I've taken one of my favorite Italian comfort food classics and created a chicken wing recipe. They are bursting with flavor, tender, juicy, cheesy and paired with my Creamy Garlic Dipping Sauce. That's *amore*! Be sure to make extra, they'll disappear fast.

SERVINGS: 4

2 lb (907 g) chicken wings, tips removed, drums and flats separated

½ cup (120 ml) marinara sauce

¾ cup (85 g) shredded mozzarella cheese

¼ cup (30 g) grated Parmesan cheese

MARINADE

2 tbsp (30 ml) extra-virgin olive oil

½ tbsp (7 ml) balsamic vinegar

1 tsp garlic powder

1 tsp onion powder

1 tsp Italian seasoning

½ tsp oregano

1 tsp paprika

Salt and pepper, to taste

CREAMY GARLIC DIPPING SAUCE

½ cup (120 ml) Caesar dressing

2 tbsp (15 g) grated Parmesan cheese

¼ cup (60 ml) mayonnaise

4 cloves garlic, minced

1 tsp parsley flakes

¼ tsp black pepper

FOR SERVING

1 tbsp (3 g) chopped fresh basil

Crushed red pepper flakes

Creamy Garlic Dipping Sauce

With a paper towel, pat the wings dry. Place the wings in a shallow dish or resealable plastic bag. Make the marinade. In a medium bowl, whisk together the olive oil, balsamic vinegar, garlic powder, onion powder, Italian seasoning, oregano, paprika, salt and pepper. Pour the marinade over the wings and toss to coat. Cover or seal and refrigerate for 2 hours or overnight (the longer the better).

Preheat the grill or smoker to 350°F (180°C), indirect heat.

Grill the wings for 40 minutes or until they reach a minimum internal temperature of 165°F (75°C), or 190°F (90°C) if you like them well-done, flipping them halfway through the cooking time. To crisp the skin, move the wings to the direct heat side of the grill, turning occasionally, until the skin is dark golden or to your liking.

Meanwhile, prepare the dipping sauce. In a medium bowl, combine the Caesar dressing, Parmesan cheese, mayonnaise, garlic, parsley flakes and pepper. Cover and refrigerate until ready to serve.

Turn the grill up to 400°F (200°C). Place the wings on a lined baking tray or cast-iron skillet. Top with the marinara sauce, mozzarella cheese and Parmesan cheese. Place them back on the grill for 5 to 10 minutes or until the cheese has melted.

Plate the wings and garnish them with the basil and red pepper flakes. Serve them with the Creamy Garlic Dipping Sauce.

BIRRIA STYLE

Birria tacos have become a super popular recipe and consist of braised meat in sweet, sour, slightly spicy and utterly savory Mexican flavors. These chicken wings have all those familiar flavors and will quickly become one of your favorites. This recipe is simple to make, and you'll even have leftover consommé (sauce) to make tacos.

SERVINGS: 4

2 lb (907 g) chicken wings, tips removed, drums and flats separated

1 tsp garlic powder

1 tsp onion powder

1 tsp paprika

1 tbsp (6 g) cumin

1 tbsp (6 g) ground coriander

1 tsp oregano

1 tsp ground ginger

1/8 tsp cinnamon (optional)

1 tsp crushed red pepper flakes, or to taste

1/2 tsp white pepper

Salt and black pepper, to taste

1 tsp vegetable oil

BIRRIA-STYLE SAUCE (CONSOMMÉ)

6 cups (1.4 L) water, divided, plus more as needed

2 dried pasilla peppers, stems and seeds removed

2 dried guajillo peppers, stems and seeds removed

2 dried ancho chilies, stems and seeds removed

1 tbsp (15 ml) vegetable oil

1 medium white onion, diced

6 cloves garlic, minced

3¾ cups (900 ml) low-sodium beef stock

2 basil leaves

2 chipotle peppers in adobo sauce

2 tbsp (30 g) crushed tomatoes

FOR SERVING

1 tbsp (10 g) diced white onion

1 tbsp (1 g) chopped cilantro

Birria-Style Sauce

With a paper towel, pat the wings dry. Place them in a shallow dish or resealable plastic bag. In a medium bowl, combine the garlic powder, onion powder, paprika, cumin, ground coriander, oregano, ground ginger, cinnamon (if using), crushed red pepper flakes, white pepper, salt and black pepper. Toss the wings in vegetable oil and sprinkle some of the prepared rub, 2 to 3 tablespoons (14 to 21 g), over the wings, coating evenly. Set the rest aside. Cover and refrigerate for a minimum of 2 hours or overnight (the longer the better for best flavor results).

Meanwhile, prepare the sauce. In a medium pot over medium heat, add 4 cups (1 L) of water, pasilla peppers, guajillo peppers and ancho chilies. Bring to a boil. Then, cook on low for about 30 minutes. In a separate large pot over medium heat, heat the oil and add the onion and garlic. Stir frequently and sauté until the onion is translucent and the garlic is fragrant and starts to brown, 3 to 5 minutes. Next, add the beef stock, 2 cups (480 ml) of water and basil leaves. Cook for 30 minutes.

In a blender, add the pasilla peppers, guajillo peppers, ancho chilies, remaining prepared rub, chipotle peppers in adobo, crushed tomatoes and enough chili pepper water to cover the ingredients. Blend until smooth, strain and add the sauce to the pot with the beef stock and basil leaves. Stir to combine. Add any leftover chili pepper water to thin out the sauce if it's too thick for your liking. Reduce the heat to medium-low and cook for 30 to 45 minutes. Remove the basil leaves and discard.

Preheat the grill or smoker to 350°F (180°C), indirect heat.

Grill the wings for 40 minutes or until they reach a minimum internal temperature of 165°F (75°C), or 190°F (90°C) if you like them well-done, flipping them halfway through the cooking time. To crisp the skin, move the wings to the direct heat side of the grill, turning occasionally, until the skin is dark golden or to your liking. Baste the wings with the Birria-Style Sauce during the last 5 minutes.

Plate the wings and garnish them with diced onion and cilantro. Serve them with the Birria-Style Sauce for dipping.

*See image on page 52.

MAPLE PECAN PROSCIUTTO

One of my favorite cuisines is Italian and I wanted to create an Italian-style wing recipe that's beautiful and delectable. I fell in love with this recipe; it reminded me of days in Italia sitting at a café sipping on espresso and enjoying a wood-fired prosciutto pizza. These Maple Pecan Prosciutto chicken wings are sweet, crunchy and salty. You'll fall in love after one bite!

SERVINGS: 4

2 lb (907 g) chicken wings, tip removed, drums and flats separated

1 tsp garlic powder

1 tsp onion powder

1 tsp paprika

½ tsp Italian seasoning

1 tsp brown sugar

⅛ tsp cayenne pepper

Salt and pepper, to taste

1 tbsp (15 ml) extra-virgin olive oil

4 thin slices prosciutto

¼ cup (56 g) unsalted butter

1 tbsp (15 ml) maple syrup

BALSAMIC GLAZE SAUCE

½ cup (120 ml) balsamic vinegar

3 tbsp (45 ml) honey

FOR SERVING

Balsamic Glaze Sauce

Crispy prosciutto

2 tbsp (14 g) finely chopped raw pecans

2 tbsp grated (15 g) Parmesan cheese

With a paper towel, pat the wings dry. In a small bowl, combine the garlic powder, onion powder, paprika, Italian seasoning, brown sugar, cayenne, salt and pepper. Toss the wings in the olive oil and sprinkle the prepared rub over the wings, coating evenly.

Preheat the grill or smoker to 350°F (180°C), indirect heat.

Place the prosciutto slices on a lined baking tray. Do not overlap the slices. Grill with the wings (if you have space, otherwise use the oven) for 15 to 20 minutes or until the prosciutto is crispy. Place on a wire rack to cool; the prosciutto will get crispier as it cools. Once cooled, crumble it into bite-sized pieces.

Grill the wings for 40 minutes or until they reach a minimum internal temperature of 165°F (75°C), or 190°F (90°C) if you like them well done, flipping them halfway through the cooking time. To crisp the skin, move the wings to the direct heat side of the grill, turning occasionally, until the skin is dark golden or to your liking.

Meanwhile, prepare the sauce. In a small saucepan over medium-high heat, whisk together the balsamic vinegar and honey. Once it begins to bubble, reduce the heat to medium-low and simmer for 5 to 10 minutes until reduced by half. Let cool before using.

Transfer the wings to a bowl and top with butter and maple syrup and toss until completely coated. Plate the wings and drizzle with the Balsamic Glaze Sauce. Garnish wings with crispy prosciutto, pecans and Parmesan cheese.

CARNE ASADA STYLE

Carne Asada is a dish of grilled beef that is marinated in orange juice, olive oil, cilantro, garlic and a few more ingredients, and it's one of my favorites for tacos. This recipe involves similar ingredients with all the authentic Mexican flavors. They are juicy, tender, bright, spicy and paired with a Salsa Verde Dipping Sauce for a perfect finish!

SERVINGS: 4

2 lb (907 g) chicken wings, tips removed, drums and flats separated

CARNE ASADA MARINADE
Juice of 2 limes

4 cloves garlic, minced

½ cup (120 ml) orange juice

1 cup (8 g) chopped cilantro

¼ cup (60 ml) extra-virgin olive oil

2 tbsp (30 ml) white vinegar

¼ tsp cumin

¼ tsp smoked paprika

¼ tsp chili powder

¼ tsp onion powder

½ tsp salt, or to taste

¼ tsp black pepper, or to taste

Few splashes of Tabasco® Green Jalapeño hot sauce or 1 diced fresh jalapeño

SALSA VERDE DIPPING SAUCE
1½ lb (660 g) tomatillos, husked and halved

1–2 serrano chilies or 1–4 jalapeño peppers

1 medium white onion, diced

3 cloves garlic

¼ cup (4 g) packed fresh cilantro

1½ tbsp (22 ml) freshly squeezed lime juice, or to taste

½ tsp cumin

½ tsp salt, or to taste

FOR SERVING
1 tbsp (1 g) chopped cilantro

Lime wedges

Salsa Verde Dipping Sauce

With a paper towel, pat the wings dry. Place the wings in a shallow dish or resealable plastic bag. In a large bowl, whisk together the lime juice, garlic, orange juice, cilantro, olive oil, vinegar, cumin, smoked paprika, chili powder, onion powder, salt, pepper and hot sauce. Pour the marinade over the wings and toss to coat. Cover and refrigerate for a minimum of 4 hours or overnight.

Meanwhile, prepare the dipping sauce. Preheat the grill or smoker to 250°F (121°C). Place the tomatillos, chilies, onion and garlic on a lined baking sheet. Cook for about 30 minutes. Let cool for a few minutes. Turn the grill temperature up to 350°F (180°C) for the chicken wings. Place the cooked ingredients in a blender along with the cilantro, lime juice, cumin and salt. Blend until pureed.

Grill the wings for 40 minutes or until they reach a minimum internal temperature of 165°F (75°C), or 190°F (90°C) if you like them well done, flipping them halfway through the cooking time. To crisp the skin, move the wings to the direct heat side of the grill, turning occasionally, until the skin is dark golden or to your liking.

Plate the wings and garnish them with cilantro and serve them with lime wedges and Salsa Verde Dipping Sauce.

* See image on page 76 (shown on the top right).

BACON WRAPPED

Bacon wrapped chicken wings! Do I have your attention? I love bacon and there's nothing I wouldn't wrap in it . . . okay, maybe there are a few things, but wings aren't it. Bacon makes everything better, am I right or am I right? These wings are sweet, smoky and finished off in a delicious BBQ sauce mixture. Get out the napkins and bring your appetite!

SERVINGS: 4

2 lb (907 g) chicken wings, tips removed, drums and flats separated

1 tsp garlic powder

1 tsp onion powder

1 tsp paprika

1 tsp chili powder

1 tsp brown sugar

Salt and pepper, to taste

15 slices thin-cut bacon, halved

BBQ SAUCE GLAZE

¼ cup (60 ml) your favorite BBQ sauce

2 tbsp (30 ml) pineapple juice

1 tbsp (15 ml) apple cider vinegar

1 tbsp (15 ml) honey

1 tsp Dijon mustard

½ tsp crushed red pepper flakes

FOR SERVING

2 tbsp (12 g) chopped green onion

Ranch or blue cheese dressing

Carrot and celery sticks

Place an oven-safe baking/cooling rack on top of a parchment-lined baking sheet.

With a paper towel, pat the wings dry. In a small bowl, combine the garlic powder, onion powder, paprika, chili powder, brown sugar, salt and pepper. Sprinkle the prepared rub over the wings, coating evenly. Wrap each wing with half of a slice of bacon and place it seam side down on the prepared baking/cooling rack evenly spaced.

Meanwhile, prepare the glaze. In a small bowl, whisk to combine the BBQ sauce, pineapple juice, apple cider vinegar, honey, Dijon mustard and crushed red pepper flakes. Set aside.

Preheat the grill or smoker to 350°F (180°C), indirect heat. Place the oven-safe baking/cooling rack with the wings directly on the grill grates.

Grill the wings for 40 minutes or until they reach a minimum internal temperature of 165°F (75°C), or 190°F (90°C) if you like them well done. Make sure that the bacon is golden and crispy. There is no need to flip the wings. Baste them with BBQ Sauce Glaze during the last 5 minutes.

Plate the wings and garnish them with green onion. Serve them with ranch or blue cheese dressing for dipping and carrot and celery sticks.

* See image on page 76 (shown on the bottom).

MOM'S RECIPE

The simple things are sometimes the most significant, and these chicken wings are just that. They're simple, flavorful and one of my most requested recipes. These wings are garlicky and double-tossed in sauce, plus my mom always goes heavy on the salt and pepper. Adjust to your preference and share some memories with loved ones.

SERVINGS: 4

2 lb (907 g) chicken wings, tips removed, drums and flats separated

Kraft® Chicken 'n Rib Sauce or your favorite BBQ sauce

MOM'S MARINADE
1 tbsp (15 ml) grapeseed oil

2 tsp (6 g) garlic powder

1 tsp paprika

3 cloves garlic, minced

1/4 tsp cayenne pepper

1–2 tbsp (14–28 g) fine Himalayan pink salt, or to taste

1 tbsp (8 g) black pepper, or to taste

FOR SERVING
1 tbsp (3 g) chopped parsley

Crushed red pepper flakes (optional)

Ranch or Caesar dressing

Carrot and celery sticks

With a paper towel, pat the wings dry. Place the wings in a shallow dish or resealable plastic bag. For Mom's Marinade, in a small bowl, whisk together the grapeseed oil, garlic powder, paprika, minced garlic, cayenne, Himalayan pink salt and black pepper. Pour the marinade over the wings and toss to coat. Cover and refrigerate for 2 hours or overnight (the longer the better for best flavor results).

Preheat the grill or smoker to 350°F (180°C), indirect heat.

Grill the wings for 40 minutes or until they reach a minimum internal temperature of 165°F (75°C), or 190°F (90°C) if you like them well done, flipping them halfway through the cooking time. To crisp the skin, move the wings to the direct heat side of the grill, turning occasionally, until the skin is dark golden or to your liking.

Transfer the wings to a bowl and toss them with the BBQ sauce until completely coated. Place the wings back on the grill grates for 5 to 10 minutes, until the sauce settles and starts to caramelize slightly.

Transfer the wings back into the bowl and toss with the BBQ sauce again, until completely coated, or serve immediately. Plate the wings and garnish them with parsley and crushed red pepper flakes, if using. Serve them with ranch or Caesar dressing for dipping and carrot and celery sticks.

SAUCE BOSS

The sauce is the boss. Finger lickin', lip smackin', hella good saucy sauce! There's a sauce for everyone ranging from mild to wild, sticky to sweet and bold flavors that take chicken wings to the next level. I like to get saucy with some of my favorite recipes, such as Spicy Chili Garlic (page 84), Mexican Buffalo (page 91), Raspberry Hoisin (page 93) and Jalapeño Cheddar (page 112). Don't be afraid to get sauce all over your face—chances are the person in front of you looks the same.

SPICY CHILI GARLIC

These sticky, sweet and spicy wings are your latest drool-worthy obsession, guaranteed. You will be asking yourself: where have these been all my life? The combination of garlic, sticky honey, soy and ginger takes these wings to a whole other level. This sauce is so incredible, you will want to double it. To do so, simply double the ingredients.

SERVINGS: 4

2 lb (907 g) chicken wings, tips removed, drums and flats separated

1 tsp garlic powder

1 tsp onion powder

1 tsp paprika

½ tsp cayenne pepper, or to taste

Salt and pepper, to taste

SPICY CHILI GARLIC SAUCE

1 tbsp (15 ml) vegetable oil

2 tsp (9 ml) sesame oil

4 whole dried red chili peppers

1 tbsp (8 g) minced garlic

1 tbsp (6 g) minced ginger

1 tsp crushed red pepper flakes

2 tbsp (30 ml) low-sodium soy sauce

2 tbsp (30 ml) rice vinegar

3 tbsp (45 ml) honey

1 tbsp (15 ml) water

FOR SERVING

Sesame seeds

2 tbsp (12 g) chopped green onion

Leftover Spicy Chili Garlic Sauce

Blue cheese or ranch dressing

With a paper towel, pat the wings dry. In a small bowl, combine the garlic powder, onion powder, paprika, cayenne, salt and pepper. Sprinkle the prepared rub over the wings, coating evenly.

Preheat the grill or smoker to 350°F (180°C), indirect heat.

Grill the wings for 40 minutes or until they reach a minimum internal temperature of 165°F (75°C), or 190°F (90°C) if you like them well done, flipping them halfway through the cooking time. To crisp the skin, move the wings to the direct heat side of the grill, turning occasionally, until the skin is dark golden or to your liking.

Meanwhile, prepare the sauce. In a small saucepan, heat the vegetable oil and sesame oil over medium heat. Add the dried red chili peppers and minced garlic and ginger. Stir frequently and sauté until the garlic and ginger start to brown, 2 to 3 minutes. Add the crushed red pepper flakes, soy sauce, rice vinegar, honey and water. Bring to a boil, then reduce heat to a simmer. Simmer for about 5 minutes or until the sauce is thickened.

Transfer the wings to a bowl and toss with the Spicy Chili Garlic Sauce until completely coated. Plate the wings and garnish them with sesame seeds and green onion. Serve them with leftover sauce and/or ranch dressing.

LEMON PEPPER GARLIC PARMESAN

2 lb (907 g) chicken wings, tips removed, drums and flats separated

1 tbsp (12 g) lemon pepper seasoning (page 25)

1 tsp paprika

GARLIC PARMESAN SAUCE

4 tbsp (56 g) unsalted butter, melted

2 cloves garlic, minced

2 tbsp (30 ml) freshly squeezed lemon juice

½ cup (45 g) grated Parmesan cheese

2 tbsp (8 g) chopped fresh parsley

FOR SERVING

Caesar or ranch dressing

These Lemon Pepper Garlic Parmesan chicken wings will be a huge hit with your family and friends! They are tender, juicy and loaded with a buttery, rich Garlic Parmesan Sauce. Best of all, they are mild enough that everyone can eat them.

SERVINGS: 4

With a paper towel, pat the wings dry. In a small bowl, combine the lemon pepper seasoning and paprika. Sprinkle the prepared rub over the wings, coating evenly.

Preheat the grill or smoker to 350°F (180°C), indirect heat.

Grill the wings for 40 minutes or until they reach a minimum internal temperature of 165°F (74°C), or 190°F (90°C) if you like them well done, flipping them halfway through the cooking time. To crisp the skin, move the wings to the direct heat side of the grill, turning occasionally, until the skin is dark golden or to your liking.

Meanwhile, prepare the sauce. In a large bowl, stir together the warm melted butter, garlic, lemon juice, Parmesan cheese and parsley. Add the wings and toss until completely coated. Serve them with Caesar or ranch dressing.

GOCHUJANG

2 lb (907 g) chicken wings, tips removed, drums and flats separated

¼ cup (60 ml) low-sodium soy sauce

3–4 tbsp (45–60 ml) gochujang chili paste (or sriracha)

1 tbsp (7 g) crushed red pepper flakes

1 tbsp (15 ml) rice vinegar

3 tbsp (45 ml) honey

1 tbsp (8 g) minced garlic

1 tbsp (6 g) minced ginger

Salt and pepper, to taste

GOCHUJANG BUTTER SAUCE

2–4 tbsp (28–57 g) unsalted butter, melted

Leftover Gochujang mixture

FOR SERVING

Sesame seeds

2 tbsp (12 g) chopped green onion

Leftover Gochujang Butter Sauce

These Korean Gochujang chicken wings are sweet, savory and spicy, and they are finished off in a rich buttery sauce. They are not as spicy as you may think, so don't worry, you won't need an extinguisher to put out a fire in your mouth. Don't skip the gochujang paste, it adds this umami flavor that you simply can't get from a hot sauce.

SERVINGS: 4

With a paper towel, pat the wings dry. Place the wings in a large mixing bowl. In a medium bowl, whisk together the soy sauce, gochujang, crushed red pepper flakes, rice vinegar, honey, garlic, ginger, salt and pepper. Pour some of the mixture on the wings, enough to just coat. Keep the rest aside to make the Gochujang Butter Sauce. Set the wings aside for 20 minutes and up to 1 hour, refrigerated.

Preheat the grill or smoker to 350°F (180°C), indirect heat.

Grill the wings for 40 minutes or until they reach a minimum internal temperature of 165°F (75°C), or 190°F (90°C) if you like them well done, flipping them halfway through the cooking time. To crisp the skin, move the wings to the direct heat side of the grill, turning occasionally, until the skin is dark golden or to your liking.

Meanwhile, prepare the sauce. In a large bowl, stir together the warm melted butter and the remaining Gochujang mixture. Add the wings and toss until completely coated. Place them back on the grill grates for 5 to 10 minutes, until the sauce settles, or serve immediately. Plate the wings and garnish them with sesame seeds and green onion. Serve them with the leftover Gochujang Butter Sauce.

HONEY BBQ

These chicken wings are tender, juicy and smothered in a sweet and spicy Honey BBQ Sauce. They are a classic that everyone will love at a party, game day, backyard BBQ or weeknight meal. This sauce is perfect to prepare ahead of time and warm up. You'll be giving out this recipe in no time.

SERVINGS: 4

2 lb (907 g) chicken wings, tips removed, drums and flats separated

1 tsp garlic powder

1 tsp onion powder

1 tsp paprika

¼ tsp chili powder

¼ tsp cayenne pepper

2 tsp (10 g) brown sugar

1 tsp cornstarch

Salt and pepper, to taste

HONEY BBQ SAUCE

¼ cup (60 ml) ketchup

1–2 tbsp (15–30 ml) apple cider vinegar

1 tbsp (15 ml) Worcestershire sauce

1 tsp low-sodium soy sauce

4 tbsp (60 ml) honey

1 tsp smoked paprika

1 tsp garlic powder

1 tsp onion powder

¼ cup (60 ml) hot sauce, or to taste (I use Frank's RedHot Original)

Salt and pepper, to taste

FOR SERVING

2 tbsp (12 g) chopped green onion

Ranch or blue cheese dressing

Carrot and celery sticks

With a paper towel, pat the wings dry. In a small bowl, combine the garlic powder, onion powder, paprika, chili powder, cayenne, brown sugar, cornstarch, salt and pepper. Sprinkle the prepared rub over the wings, coating evenly.

Preheat the grill or smoker to 350°F (180°C), indirect heat.

Grill the wings for 40 minutes or until they reach a minimum internal temperature of 165°F (75°C), or 190°F (90°C) if you like them well done, flipping them halfway through the cooking time. To crisp the skin, move the wings to the direct heat side of the grill, turning occasionally, until the skin is dark golden or to your liking.

Meanwhile, prepare the sauce. In a large saucepan over medium heat, whisk together the ketchup, apple cider vinegar, Worcestershire sauce, soy sauce, honey, smoked paprika, garlic powder, onion powder, hot sauce, salt and pepper. Bring to a boil, stirring occasionally. Reduce heat to low and simmer for about 5 minutes or until the sauce reduces and thickens, stirring frequently.

Transfer the wings to a bowl and toss with Honey BBQ Sauce until completely coated. Place the wings back on the grill grates for 5 to 10 minutes, until the sauce settles, or serve immediately. Plate the wings and garnish them with green onion. Serve them with ranch or blue cheese dressing for dipping and carrot and celery sticks.

*See image on page 89 (shown on the top left).

MEXICAN BUFFALO

I love Mexican cuisine and these wings are one of my favorite flavor combos! You'll taste some of the familiar flavors such as cumin, chili powder and cayenne pepper. They are spicy, buttery, zesty and a handheld guilty pleasure paired with my Cilantro Crema Dipping Sauce. If you're a fan of traditional Buffalo wings, these are a must try! You won't be disappointed.

SERVINGS: 4

2 lb (907 g) chicken wings, tips removed, drums and flats separated

½ tbsp (4 g) garlic powder

½ tbsp (4 g) onion powder

1 tbsp (7 g) smoked paprika or sweet paprika

½ tbsp (4 g) chili powder

½ tsp cumin

½ tsp cayenne pepper

Salt and pepper, to taste

CILANTRO CREMA DIPPING SAUCE

¼ cup (60 ml) mayonnaise

¼ cup (60 ml) sour cream

1 tbsp (7 g) chili powder

1 tbsp (7 g) garlic powder

1 tbsp (7 g) onion powder

1 tbsp (15 ml) lime juice

2 tbsp (14 g) crumbled Cotija or feta cheese

1 tbsp (1 g) chopped cilantro

Splash of Valentina® Mexican Hot Sauce

MEXICAN BUFFALO SAUCE

4 tbsp (56 g) unsalted butter

1 tbsp (15 ml) honey

½ cup (120 ml) Valentina Mexican Hot Sauce

FOR SERVING

Cilantro Crema Dipping Sauce

Lime wedges

With a paper towel, pat the wings dry. In a small bowl, combine the garlic powder, onion powder, smoked paprika, chili powder, cumin, cayenne, salt and pepper. Sprinkle the prepared rub over the wings, coating evenly.

Preheat the grill or smoker to 350°F (180°C), indirect heat.

Grill the wings for 40 minutes or until they reach a minimum internal temperature of 165°F (75°C), or 190°F (90°C) if you like them well done, flipping them halfway through the cooking time. To crisp the skin, move the wings to the direct heat side of the grill, turning occasionally, until the skin is dark golden or to your liking.

Meanwhile, prepare the dipping sauce. In a small bowl, combine the mayonnaise, sour cream, chili powder, garlic powder, onion powder, lime juice, Cotija or feta cheese, cilantro and Valentina hot sauce.

Transfer the wings to a bowl and top with the butter, honey and Valentina hot sauce. Toss until completely coated. Plate and serve them with Cilantro Crema Dipping Sauce and lime wedges.

*See image on page 89 (shown on the bottom).

RASPBERRY HOISIN

These Asian-style sweet, spicy and sticky chicken wings will quickly disappear off the plate, so be sure to make some extra. The marrying of garlic, ginger, hoisin and raspberry jam in the sauce makes a beautiful aroma and incredible flavor combo. If you're not a fan of too much spice, these wings taste just as incredible without the added cayenne pepper and sriracha sauce.

SERVINGS: 4

2 lb (907 g) chicken wings, tips removed, drums and flats separated
1 tbsp (15 ml) sesame oil
1 tsp hoisin sauce
1 tsp paprika
1 tsp garlic powder
1 tsp onion powder
½ tsp cayenne pepper
1 tbsp (5 g) Chinese five-spice
Salt and pepper, to taste

RASPBERRY HOISIN SAUCE
2 tsp (10 ml) low-sodium soy sauce
1 tsp rice vinegar
⅓ cup (80 ml) hoisin sauce
1 tsp sriracha
¼ cup (60 ml) seedless raspberry jam (or blackberry jam)
¼ tsp minced garlic
¼ tsp minced ginger

FOR SERVING
Sesame seeds
2 tbsp (12 g) chopped green onion
Leftover Raspberry Hoisin Sauce

With a paper towel, pat the wings dry. Place the wings in a shallow dish or resealable plastic bag. In a medium bowl, whisk together the sesame oil, hoisin sauce, paprika, garlic powder, onion powder, cayenne, Chinese five-spice, salt and pepper. Pour the marinade over the wings and toss to coat. Set aside for 20 minutes and up to 1 hour in the refrigerator.

Preheat the grill or smoker to 350°F (180°C), indirect heat.

Grill the wings for 40 minutes or until they reach a minimum internal temperature of 165°F (75°C), or 190°F (90°C) if you like them well done, flipping them halfway through the cooking time. To crisp the skin, move the wings to the direct heat side of the grill, turning occasionally, until the skin is dark golden or to your liking.

Meanwhile, prepare the sauce. In a small saucepan over medium-low heat, whisk together the soy sauce, rice vinegar, hoisin sauce, sriracha, raspberry jam, garlic and ginger. Stir frequently and bring to a boil.

Transfer the wings to a bowl and toss with the Raspberry Hoisin Sauce until completely coated. Plate and garnish them with sesame seeds and green onion. Serve them with the leftover sauce for dipping.

CAJUN BUFFALO

This chicken wing recipe combines my love for a dry rub and hot sauce. Cajun and Buffalo = Cajuffalo. Most times I'm debating between these two flavors, so why not combine them? These wings are saucy, tender, juicy and have the perfect amount of heat! Once you make your first batch, you'll be making them over and over again. The requests will keep on coming.

SERVINGS: 4

2 lb (907 g) chicken wings, tips removed, drums and flats separated

1½ tbsp (10 g) paprika

1 tbsp (8 g) garlic powder

½ tbsp (4 g) onion powder

½ tbsp (3 g) cayenne powder

¼ tsp red pepper flakes

1 tsp dried thyme

1 tsp dried oregano

½ tbsp (4 g) chili powder

½ tbsp (3 g) black pepper

½ tsp white pepper

½ tsp kosher salt, or to taste

½ tbsp (4 g) minced garlic

2 tbsp (28 g) unsalted butter

½ cup (120 ml) Frank's RedHot Original

CAJUN RANCH DIPPING SAUCE

½ cup (120 ml) ranch dressing

¼ cup (60 ml) mayonnaise

½ tbsp (4 g) prepared Cajun rub

FOR SERVING

2 tbsp (12 g) chopped green onion

Cajun Ranch Dipping Sauce

Carrot and celery sticks

With a paper towel, pat the wings dry. In a small bowl, combine the paprika, garlic powder, onion powder, cayenne, red pepper flakes, thyme, oregano, chili powder, black pepper, white pepper and salt. Sprinkle about 3 tablespoons (21 g) of the prepared rub over the wings, coating evenly.

Preheat the grill or smoker to 350°F (180°C), indirect heat.

Grill the wings for 40 minutes or until they reach a minimum internal temperature of 165°F (75°C), or 190°F (90°C) if you like them well done, flipping them halfway through the cooking time. To crisp the skin, move the wings to the direct heat side of the grill, turning occasionally, until the skin is dark golden or to your liking.

Meanwhile, prepare the dipping sauce. In a small bowl, whisk to combine the ranch dressing, mayonnaise and prepared Cajun rub.

Transfer the wings to a bowl and top with the minced garlic, butter and hot sauce. Toss until completely coated. Plate the wings and garnish them with green onion. Serve them with Cajun Ranch Dipping Sauce and carrot and celery sticks.

*See image on page 82 (shown on the top).

LEBUFF (LEMON BUFFALO)

These LeBuff chicken wings are the next best thing since sliced bread. This combo is EVERYTHING! Lemony, peppery and tossed in a delicious buttery Buffalo sauce, these wings are insanely delicious and oh so easy to make. Make my Lemon Pepper Seasoning recipe or, to save time, use your favorite lemon pepper seasoning if you'd like.

SERVINGS: 4

2 lb (907 g) chicken wings, tips removed, drums and flats separated

1 tbsp (12 g) Lemon Pepper Seasoning (page 25)

1 tsp garlic powder

1 tsp onion powder

1 tsp paprika

LEBUFF SAUCE

½ cup (120 ml) Frank's RedHot Original

½ tbsp (6 g) lemon pepper seasoning

1 tsp freshly squeezed lemon juice

2 tbsp (28 g) unsalted butter

FOR SERVING

1 tsp Lemon Pepper Seasoning (optional)

Lemon wedges

Ranch or blue cheese dressing

Carrot and celery stick

With a paper towel, pat the wings dry. In a small bowl, combine the Lemon Pepper Seasoning, garlic powder, onion powder and paprika. Sprinkle the prepared rub over the wings, coating evenly.

Preheat the grill or smoker to 350°F (180°C), indirect heat.

Grill the wings for 40 minutes or until they reach a minimum internal temperature of 165°F (75°C), or 190°F (90°C) if you like them well done, flipping them halfway through the cooking time. To crisp the skin, move the wings to the direct heat side of the grill, turning occasionally, until the skin is dark golden or to your liking.

Meanwhile, prepare the sauce. In a small saucepan over medium-low heat, whisk together the hot sauce, Lemon Pepper Seasoning and lemon juice. Bring to a simmer, then stir in the butter. Cook until the butter is melted and slightly reduced, about 2 minutes.

Transfer the wings to a bowl and toss with the LeBuff Sauce until completely coated.

Add an optional extra teaspoon of Lemon Pepper Seasoning to the coated wings. Plate the wings and serve them with lemon wedges, ranch or blue cheese dressing and carrot and celery sticks.

*See image on page 82 (shown on the right).

FLAMIN' HOT DILL

Have you tried the Flamin' Dill potato chips? Well, these saucy chicken wings have all those familiar flavors. They are brined in pickle juice and pickled jalapeño juice to make them tender, juicy and spicy. Oooooh and that Flamin' Hot Dill Sauce is money. These wings will blow you away.

SERVINGS: 4

2 lb (907 g) chicken wings, tips removed, drums and flats separated

FLAMIN' HOT DILL MARINADE

¼ cup (60 ml) dill pickle juice (the liquid from a jar of pickles)

¼ cup (60 ml) pickling juice from pickled jalapeños

FLAMIN' HOT DILL RUB

1 tsp dried dill

1 tsp smoked paprika

1 tsp brown sugar

½ tsp garlic powder

1 tsp onion powder

½ tsp cayenne pepper

1 tsp chipotle powder

1 tsp tomato soup mix powder (I use Knorr)

Salt and pepper, to taste

FLAMIN' HOT DILL SAUCE

¼ cup (56 g) unsalted butter

½ cup (120 ml) Frank's RedHot Original

1 tsp Tabasco hot sauce

½ tsp fresh chopped dill

2 tsp (6 g) garlic powder

1 tsp onion powder

Black pepper, to taste

FOR SERVING

2 tbsp (12 g) chopped green onion

Ranch or blue cheese dressing

Carrot and celery sticks

With a paper towel, pat the wings dry. Place the wings in a shallow dish or resealable plastic bag. In a small bowl, combine the dill pickle juice and pickling juice from pickled jalapeños. Pour the marinade over the wings and toss to coat. Cover and refrigerate for 4 hours or overnight (the longer the better for best flavor results).

In a small bowl, combine the dried dill, smoked paprika, brown sugar, garlic powder, onion powder, cayenne, chipotle powder, tomato soup powder, salt and pepper. Remove the wings from the marinade and with a paper towel, pat them dry. Discard the marinade. Sprinkle the prepared rub over the wings, coating evenly.

Preheat the grill or smoker to 350°F (180°C), indirect heat.

Grill the wings for 40 minutes or until they reach a minimum internal temperature of 165°F (75°C), or 190°F (90°C) if you like them well done, flipping them halfway through the cooking time. To crisp the skin, move the wings to the direct heat side of the grill, turning occasionally, until the skin is dark golden or to your liking.

Meanwhile, prepare the sauce. In a small saucepan over medium heat, melt the butter and whisk together Frank's RedHot sauce, Tabasco, dill, garlic powder, onion powder and black pepper. Bring to a boil and reduce the heat to low. Simmer for 2 to 3 minutes.

Transfer the wings to a bowl and toss with Flamin' Hot Dill Sauce until completely coated. Place the wings back on the grill grates for about 5 minutes, until the sauce settles, or serve immediately. Plate the wings and garnish them with green onion. Serve them with ranch or blue cheese dressing for dipping and carrot and celery sticks.

*See image on page 82 (shown on the left).

SRIRACHA HONEY

All it takes is one bite to fall in love with these wings. Dial the heat up or down depending on your preference. They are easy to make and perfect for busy weeknights or to serve a crowd. Make the sauce ahead of time and warm it up when you're ready to toss the wings. Top them with sesame seeds and green onion for the finishing touch.

SERVINGS: 4

2 lb (907 g) chicken wings, tips removed, drums and flats separated

1 tsp garlic powder

1 tsp onion powder

1 tsp paprika

1 tsp brown sugar

1/8 tsp cayenne pepper

Salt and pepper, to taste

1/2 tbsp (7 ml) sesame oil

SRIRACHA HONEY SAUCE

1 tbsp (15 ml) low-sodium soy sauce

2–4 tsp (10–20 ml) sriracha, or to taste

1/4 cup (60 ml) honey

1 tsp rice vinegar

1/4 cup (50 g) brown sugar

1 tbsp (15 ml) ketchup

Juice of 1 lime

FOR SERVING

Sesame seeds

2 tbsp (12 g) chopped green onion

Leftover Sriracha Honey Sauce

Ranch dressing (optional)

With a paper towel, pat the wings dry. In a small bowl, combine the garlic powder, onion powder, paprika, brown sugar, cayenne, salt and pepper. Toss the wings in the sesame oil and sprinkle the prepared rub over the wings, coating evenly.

Preheat the grill or smoker to 350°F (180°C), indirect heat.

Grill the wings for 40 minutes or until they reach a minimum internal temperature of 165°F (75°C), or 190°F (90°C) if you like them well done, flipping them halfway through the cooking time. To crisp the skin, move the wings to the direct heat side of the grill, turning occasionally, until the skin is dark golden or to your liking.

Meanwhile, prepare the sauce. In a small saucepan over medium heat, whisk together the soy sauce, sriracha, honey, rice vinegar, brown sugar, ketchup and lime juice. Bring to a boil, stirring frequently. Reduce heat to low and simmer for about 2 minutes until the sauce has thickened.

Transfer the wings to a bowl and toss with the Sriracha Honey Sauce until completely coated. Plate the wings and garnish them with sesame seeds and green onion. Serve them with leftover sauce and/or ranch dressing.

HALFTIME HOISIN

It's game day and it's halftime, what are you snacking on? Wings of course! I've got a flat in one hand and a drumette in the other. The sheer aroma of these is hypnotizing, which one should I take a bite of first? The correct answer is … it doesn't matter because they both taste equally delicious! These are sticky, sweet, with a hint of spice and the perfect finger food. No dipping sauce required; these Halftime Hoisin wings have all the flavor you need.

SERVINGS: 4

2 lb (907 g) chicken wings, tips removed, drums and flats separated

1 tbsp (15 ml) sesame oil

½ tbsp (7 ml) hoisin sauce

1 tbsp (8 g) garlic powder

1 tsp minced ginger

1 tsp paprika

Salt and pepper, to taste

HALFTIME HOISIN SAUCE

¼ cup (60 ml) hoisin sauce

2 tbsp (30 ml) fish sauce

1 tbsp (15 ml) water

2 tbsp (30 ml) rice wine vinegar

2 tbsp (30 ml) low-sodium soy sauce

2 tbsp (30 ml) mirin

1 tbsp (15 ml) sriracha

2 tbsp (30 ml) honey

½ tbsp (4 g) minced garlic

1 tsp minced ginger

FOR SERVING

Sesame seeds

2 tbsp (12 g) chopped green onion

With a paper towel, pat the wings dry. Place the wings in a shallow dish or resealable plastic bag. In a medium bowl, whisk together the sesame oil, hoisin sauce, garlic powder, ginger, paprika, salt and pepper. Pour the marinade over the wings and toss to coat. Cover and refrigerate for 20 minutes and up to 1 hour.

Preheat the grill or smoker to 350°F (180°C), indirect heat.

Grill the wings for 40 minutes or until they reach a minimum internal temperature of 165°F (75°C), or 190°F (90°C) if you like them well done, flipping them halfway through the cooking time. To crisp the skin, move the wings to the direct heat side of the grill, turning occasionally, until the skin is dark golden or to your liking.

Meanwhile, prepare the sauce. In a small saucepan over medium heat, whisk together the hoisin sauce, fish sauce, water, rice wine vinegar, soy sauce, mirin, sriracha, honey, garlic and ginger. Stir frequently and bring to a boil. Turn the heat down and simmer for 5 to 10 minutes, or until the sauce thickens.

Transfer the wings to a bowl and toss with the Halftime Hoisin Sauce until completely coated. Plate and garnish them with sesame seeds and green onion.

BANG BANG

These chicken wings are inspired by the classic bang bang shrimp from Asian restaurants. They have all those tantalizing flavors and are easy to make for your next get-together or weeknight meal. They are tossed in a creamy, sweet, spicy chili sauce for a lip-smacking finish. This sauce is perfect for dipping.

SERVINGS: 4

BANG BANG SAUCE

½ cup (120 ml) mayonnaise

½ cup (120 ml) sweet Thai chili sauce

1 tbsp (15 ml) honey

1–2 tsp (5–10 ml) sriracha, or to taste

Salt and pepper, to taste

2 lb (907 g) chicken wings, tips removed, drums and flats separated

1 tsp garlic powder

1 tsp onion powder

1 tsp paprika

2 tsp (10 g) brown sugar

⅛ tsp cayenne pepper

¼ tsp chili powder

1 tsp cornstarch

Salt and pepper, to taste

FOR SERVING

Leftover Bang Bang Sauce

2 tbsp (12 g) chopped green onion

Ranch or blue cheese dressing (optional)

Carrot and celery sticks

Prepare the sauce. In a small bowl, whisk to combine the mayonnaise, sweet Thai chili sauce, honey, sriracha, salt and pepper.

With a paper towel, pat the wings dry. In a small bowl, combine the garlic powder, onion powder, paprika, brown sugar, cayenne, chili powder, cornstarch, salt and pepper. Sprinkle the prepared rub over the wings, coating evenly. Add 1 to 2 tablespoons (15 to 30 ml) of Bang Bang Sauce to the wings and toss to coat evenly.

Preheat the grill or smoker to 375°F (191°C), indirect heat.

Grill the wings for 40 minutes or until they reach a minimum internal temperature of 165°F (75°C), or 190°F (90°C) if you like them well done, flipping them halfway through the cooking time. To crisp the skin, move the wings to the direct heat side of the grill, turning occasionally, until the skin is dark golden or to your liking.

Transfer the wings to a bowl and toss them with more Bang Bang Sauce until completely coated. Place wings back on the grill grates for about 5 minutes, until the sauce settles. Plate the wings and garnish them with green onion and drizzle on some more sauce, if desired. Serve them with leftover sauce and/or ranch or blue cheese dressing for dipping and carrot and celery sticks.

*See image on page 101 (shown on the bottom left).

TRUFFLE PARMESAN

Oh, you fancy, huh? These Truffle Parmesan chicken wings will blow your mind. The beautiful combo of truffle oil, butter, garlic and Parmesan is sure to be a crowd-pleaser. They are simple to make and will quickly disappear. Make these for dinner, at your next get-together or backyard BBQ. Enjoy with a cold beer or a glass of wine.

SERVINGS: 4

2 lb (907 g) chicken wings, tips removed, drums and flats separated

1 tsp garlic powder

1 tsp onion powder

1 tsp paprika

½ tsp grated Parmesan cheese

Salt and pepper, to taste

1 tbsp (15 ml) truffle oil

TRUFFLE BUTTER SAUCE

8 tbsp (112 g) unsalted butter

2 cloves garlic, minced

2 tsp (10 ml) truffle oil

A few splashes of your favorite hot sauce (I use Frank's RedHot Original)

½ cup (50 g) grated Parmesan cheese

Salt and pepper, to taste

FOR SERVING

2 tbsp (8 g) chopped parsley

Ranch or blue cheese dressing

With a paper towel, pat the wings dry. In a small bowl, combine the garlic powder, onion powder, paprika, Parmesan cheese, salt and pepper. Toss the wings in the truffle oil and sprinkle the prepared rub over the wings, coating evenly. Refrigerate for 20 minutes and up to 1 hour.

Preheat the grill or smoker to 350°F (180°C), indirect heat.

Grill the wings for 40 minutes or until they reach a minimum internal temperature of 165°F (75°C), or 190°F (90°C) if you like them well done, flipping them halfway through the cooking time. To crisp the skin, move the wings to the direct heat side of the grill, turning occasionally, until the skin is dark golden or to your liking.

Meanwhile, prepare the sauce. In a small saucepan over medium-low heat, add the butter and garlic. Simmer for about 2 minutes until the garlic is soft and fragrant. In a large bowl, stir together the melted garlic butter, truffle oil, hot sauce, Parmesan cheese, salt and pepper. Add the wings and toss until completely coated. Plate the wings and garnish them with parsley. Serve them with ranch or blue cheese dressing.

*See image on page 101 (shown on the bottom right).

BLACKBERRY JALAPEÑO

Take your chicken wings to the next level with this bold flavor pairing that creates a deep purple blackberry sauce. Dig right in and don't be afraid to wear some sauce on your face. No one will notice, they'll be too busy pigging out on these irresistibly delicious wings. Serve them with wet naps—it will get saucy.

SERVINGS: 4

2 lb (907 g) chicken wings, tips removed, drums and flats separated

1 tsp garlic powder

1 tsp onion powder

½ tsp paprika

1 tsp cornstarch

Salt and pepper, to taste

BLACKBERRY JALAPEÑO SAUCE

2 tbsp (30 ml) vegetable oil

2 cloves garlic, minced

½ onion, chopped

1 jalapeño, chopped

2 cups (325 g) fresh or frozen blackberries

¼ cup (60 ml) honey

1 tsp balsamic vinegar

Salt and pepper, to taste

2 tbsp (30 ml) water (optional)

FOR SERVING

2 tbsp (12 g) chopped green onion

Fresh blackberries

Leftover Blackberry Jalapeño Sauce

Ranch or blue cheese dressing (optional)

Carrot and celery sticks

With a paper towel, pat the wings dry. In a small bowl, combine the garlic powder, onion powder, paprika, cornstarch, salt and pepper. Sprinkle the prepared rub over the wings, coating evenly.

Preheat the grill or smoker to 350°F (180°C), indirect heat.

Grill the wings for 40 minutes or until they reach a minimum internal temperature of 165°F (75°C), or 190°F (90°C) if you like them well done, flipping them halfway through the cooking time. To crisp the skin, move the wings to the direct heat side of the grill, turning occasionally, until the skin is dark golden or to your liking.

Meanwhile, prepare the sauce. In a medium saucepan over medium heat, add the oil, garlic, onion and jalapeño. Cook until softened, 4 to 5 minutes, stirring occasionally. Add in the blackberries, honey, balsamic vinegar, salt and pepper. Bring to a simmer until the blackberries are hot and the sauce is bubbling, about 5 minutes, stirring frequently. Add water if the sauce is too thick for your liking. Place the sauce in a blender and puree on high until smooth. Strain the sauce over a bowl if you'd like a smoother sauce.

Transfer the wings to a bowl and toss with the Blackberry Jalapeño Sauce until completely coated. Plate the wings and garnish them with green onion. Serve them with fresh blackberries, leftover sauce and/or ranch or blue cheese dressing for dipping and carrot and celery sticks.

SWEET 'N' SPICY PEACH

Cue "I got my peaches out in Georgia (oh, yeah…)." These Sweet 'n' Spicy Peach wings are so incredibly delicious that you won't be able to stop eating them, and the best part is, they are easy to prepare. This sauce is sticky, mouthwatering and a must for dipping. Adjust the heat level to your preference.

SERVINGS: 4

2 lb (907 g) chicken wings, tips removed, drums and flats separated

1 tsp paprika

1 tsp garlic powder

1 tsp onion powder

¼ tsp chili powder

¼ tsp cayenne

2 tsp (10 g) brown sugar

Salt and pepper, to taste

SWEET 'N' SPICY PEACH SAUCE

½ (12-oz [398-ml]) can sliced peaches in syrup plus 2 tbsp (30 ml) of syrup

2 tbsp (30 ml) peach jam

¼ cup (60 ml) Hellmann's® Smoked Peach Vinaigrette or ½ tbsp (7 ml) apple cider vinegar

1 clove garlic, minced

1 tsp Tabasco or your favorite hot sauce, or to taste

Salt and pepper, to taste

FOR SERVING

2 tbsp (12 g) chopped green onion

Leftover Sweet 'n' Spicy Peach Sauce

Carrot and celery sticks

With a paper towel, pat the wings dry. In a small bowl, combine the paprika, garlic powder, onion powder, chili powder, cayenne, brown sugar, salt and pepper. Sprinkle the prepared rub over the wings, coating evenly.

Preheat the grill or smoker to 350°F (180°C), indirect heat.

Grill the wings for 40 minutes or until they reach a minimum internal temperature of 165°F (75°C), or 190°F (90°C) if you like them well done, flipping them halfway through the cooking time. To crisp the skin, move the wings to the direct heat side of the grill, turning occasionally, until the skin is dark golden or to your liking.

Meanwhile, prepare the sauce. In a blender, place the peaches and syrup, peach jam, smoked peach dressing, garlic, hot sauce, salt and pepper. Puree on high speed for 30 to 60 seconds, until smooth. Add the peach mixture to a large saucepan and bring to a boil over medium-high heat. Reduce the heat to low and simmer for 10 to 15 minutes or until the sauce has thickened.

Transfer the wings to a bowl and toss with Sweet 'n' Spicy Peach Sauce until completely coated. Plate the wings and garnish them with green onion. Serve them with leftover sauce and carrot and celery sticks.

STICKY APRICOT

These chicken wings are sweet, slightly spicy and perfect for any occasion. They are smothered in a sticky apricot BBQ sauce that serves great as a dipping sauce. These wings are guaranteed to be on your regular rotation once you try them.

SERVINGS: 4

2 lb (907 g) chicken wings, tips removed, drums and flats separated

1 tsp garlic powder

1 tsp onion powder

1 tsp paprika

2 tsp (10 g) brown sugar

1/8 tsp cayenne pepper

1/4 tsp chili powder

Salt and pepper, to taste

APRICOT BBQ SAUCE

1 cup (240 ml) apricot preserves/jam

1/4 cup (60 ml) ketchup

2 tsp (10 ml) low-sodium soy sauce

1/2 tbsp (7 ml) Worcestershire sauce

1 tbsp (15 ml) apple cider vinegar

2 tbsp (30 ml) water, or more

1 tsp garlic powder

1 tsp onion powder

1 tsp smoked paprika

1/4 tsp chili powder

1/4 tsp crushed red pepper flakes

Salt and pepper, to taste

FOR SERVING

2 tbsp (12 g) chopped green onion

Leftover Apricot BBQ Sauce

Ranch or blue cheese dressing (optional)

Carrot and celery sticks

With a paper towel, pat the wings dry. In a small bowl, combine the garlic powder, onion powder, paprika, brown sugar, cayenne, chili powder, salt and pepper. Sprinkle the prepared rub over the wings, coating evenly.

Preheat the grill or smoker to 350°F (180°C), indirect heat.

Grill the wings for 40 minutes or until they reach a minimum internal temperature of 165°F (75°C), or 190°F (90°C) if you like them well done, flipping them halfway through the cooking time. To crisp the skin, move the wings to the direct heat side of the grill, turning occasionally, until the skin is dark golden or to your liking.

Meanwhile, prepare the sauce. In a large saucepan over medium heat, whisk together the apricot preserves, ketchup, soy sauce, Worcestershire sauce, apple cider vinegar, water, garlic powder, onion powder, smoked paprika, chili powder, crushed red pepper flakes, salt and pepper. Bring to a boil, stirring occasionally. Reduce heat to low and simmer for 5 to 10 minutes or until the sauce reduces and thickens, stirring frequently. Add more water if the sauce is too thick for your liking.

Transfer the wings to a bowl and toss with Apricot BBQ Sauce until completely coated. Place the wings back on the grill grates for 5 to 10 minutes, until the sauce settles, or serve immediately. Plate the wings and garnish them with green onion. Serve them with leftover sauce and/or ranch or blue cheese dressing for dipping and carrot and celery sticks.

MAPLE BACON

These chicken wings are tossed in an irresistible Maple BBQ sauce and topped with candied bacon! You'll "wow" any crowd with these and have them coming back for more. Be sure to make extra as they will disappear quickly.

SERVINGS: 4

CANDIED BACON
2 tbsp (30 ml) maple syrup
2½ tbsp (30 g) brown sugar
Pepper, to taste
6 slices thin-cut bacon

2 lb (907 g) chicken wings, tips removed, drums and flats separated
2 tbsp (14 g) your favorite BBQ rub (I use Louisiana Grills Maple Walnut)

MAPLE BBQ SAUCE
½ cup (120 ml) ketchup
½ cup (120 ml) maple syrup
2 tbsp (30 ml) soy sauce
1 tbsp (15 ml) apple cider vinegar
1 tbsp (15 ml) honey
¼ cup (60 ml) bourbon whiskey (I use Maker's Mark®)
½ tbsp (4 g) minced garlic
Salt and pepper, to taste

FOR SERVING
Candied Bacon crumbles
2 tbsp (12 g) chopped green onion

To make the Candied Bacon, place an oven-safe baking/cooling rack on top of a lined baking sheet. In a small bowl, combine the maple syrup, brown sugar and pepper. Brush both sides of the bacon with the mixture. Place the bacon strips, evenly spaced, on the prepared baking rack.

With a paper towel, pat the wings dry. Sprinkle your favorite rub over the wings, coating evenly.

Preheat the grill or smoker to 350°F (180°C), indirect heat.

Place the rack with the bacon directly on the grill grates if there's room. Otherwise, bake in the oven. Cook for 20 to 30 minutes, or until it looks slightly dark. Let cool for 5 minutes and crumble with your hands.

Grill the wings for 40 minutes or until they reach a minimum internal temperature of 165°F (75°C), or 190°F (90°C) if you like them well done, flipping them halfway through the cooking time. To crisp the skin, move the wings to the direct heat side of the grill, turning occasionally, until the skin is dark golden or to your liking.

Meanwhile, prepare the sauce. In a medium saucepan over medium heat, combine the ketchup, maple syrup, soy sauce, apple cider vinegar, honey, bourbon, garlic, salt and pepper. Stir frequently and bring to a boil. Reduce the heat and simmer for 10 to 15 minutes until the sauce thickens.

Transfer the wings to a bowl and toss with the Maple BBQ Sauce until coated. Place them back on the grill grates for 5 to 10 minutes, until the sauce settles, or serve immediately. Garnish them with Candied Bacon crumbles and green onion.

JALAPEÑO CHEDDAR

It's getting hot in here … These spicy chicken wings are cheesy, tangy and buttery. Best of all, they are easy to make. What more could you ask for? This sauce is boss and has familiar buffalo sauce flavors with added cheddar cheese and bursts of heat from the jalapeño peppers. Your family and friends will be raving about these wings.

SERVINGS: 4

2 lb (907 g) chicken wings, tips removed, drums and flats separated

1 tsp paprika

¼ tsp cayenne pepper

½ tsp chili powder

1 tsp garlic powder

1 tsp onion powder

Salt and pepper, to taste

1 tbsp (8 g) cornstarch

JALAPEÑO CHEDDAR SAUCE

½ cup (120 ml) Frank's RedHot Original

4 tbsp (56 g) unsalted butter

1 tbsp (15 ml) apple cider vinegar

½ tsp Worcestershire sauce

1 tsp paprika

1 tsp crushed red pepper flakes

¼ cup (68 g) finely diced pickled jalapeños

¼ cup (60 ml) pickling juice from pickled jalapeños

½ cup (56 g) shredded cheddar cheese

Salt and pepper, to taste

FOR SERVING

Jalapeño slices

2 tbsp (12 g) chopped green onion

Leftover Jalapeño Cheddar Sauce

Ranch or blue cheese dressing (optional)

With a paper towel, pat the wings dry. In a small bowl, combine the paprika, cayenne pepper, chili powder, garlic powder, onion powder, salt and pepper. Sprinkle cornstarch on the wings and toss to combine, then season with the prepared rub, coating evenly.

Preheat the grill or smoker to 350°F (180°C), indirect heat.

Grill the wings for 40 minutes or until they reach a minimum internal temperature of 165°F (75°C), or 190°F (90°C) if you like them well done, flipping them halfway through the cooking time. To crisp the skin, move the wings to the direct heat side of the grill, turning occasionally, until the skin is dark golden or to your liking.

Meanwhile, prepare the sauce. In a small saucepan over medium-low heat, add the hot sauce and butter, stirring occasionally until the butter had melted. Next, add the apple cider vinegar, Worcestershire sauce, paprika, crushed red pepper flakes, diced pickled jalapeños and pickling juice. Bring to a simmer. Turn the heat down to low and stir in the cheddar cheese. Stir frequently until the cheese is incorporated and the sauce is smooth. Season to taste with salt and pepper.

Transfer the wings to a bowl and toss with the Jalapeño Cheddar Sauce to coat. Plate the wings and garnish them with jalapeño slices and green onion. Serve with leftover sauce and/or ranch and blue cheese dressing.

*See image on page 111 (shown on the bottom left).

HOT AND BOTHERED

Can you handle the heat? These chicken wings are hot, hot, hot. If you're a lover of spicy food, then you NEED to make these. They are full of flavor and pack a punch. Make sure to use gloves when making the sauce, especially while handling the hot peppers. Grab a beer and enjoy!

SERVINGS: 4

2 lb (907 g) chicken wings, tips removed, drums and flats separated

1 tsp cayenne pepper

1 tsp crushed red pepper flakes

1 tsp garlic powder

1 tsp onion powder

1 tsp paprika

¼ tsp chili powder

Salt and pepper, to taste

HOT AND BOTHERED SAUCE

1 cup (240 ml) Frank's RedHot Original or Tabasco

½ stick unsalted butter, melted

1 tbsp (5 g) cayenne pepper

1 tbsp (6 g) crushed red pepper flakes

1 tbsp (14 g) prepared horseradish

1 tbsp (16 g) minced fresh jalapeño

2 tsp (10 g) minced fresh habañero pepper

2 tsp (6 g) garlic powder

2 tsp (5 g) onion powder

Salt and pepper, to taste

FOR SERVING

Ranch or blue cheese dressing

Carrot and celery sticks

With a paper towel, pat the wings dry. In a small bowl, combine the cayenne, crushed red pepper flakes, garlic powder, onion powder, paprika, chili powder, salt and pepper. Sprinkle the prepared rub over the wings, coating evenly.

Preheat the grill or smoker to 350°F (180°C), indirect heat.

Grill the wings for 40 minutes or until they reach a minimum internal temperature of 165°F (75°C), or 190°F (90°C) if you like them well done, flipping them halfway through the cooking time. To crisp the skin, move the wings to the direct heat side of the grill, turning occasionally, until the skin is dark golden or to your liking.

Meanwhile, prepare the sauce. In a food processor, place the hot sauce, melted butter, cayenne pepper, crushed red pepper flakes, horseradish, jalapeño, habañero, garlic powder, onion powder, salt and pepper. Blend on medium speed until the sauce is smooth.

Transfer the wings to a bowl and toss with the Hot and Bothered Sauce until completely coated. Place the wings back on the grill grates for 5 to 10 minutes, until the sauce settles, or serve immediately. Plate the wings and serve them with ranch or blue cheese dressing for dipping and carrot and celery sticks.

*See image on page 111 (shown on the top).

WINGS AROUND THE WORLD

Let me take you on a wing world tour to Mexico, Portugal, Greece, Canada, Cuba, Italy and many more—no passport necessary! I've taken some of my favorite cuisines from around the world and created mouthwatering chicken wing recipes inspired by them. Strap in, it's going to be a wild flavor ride. Turn up the volume on your wing game with some of the best flavor combos! Some of my favorites include Poutine, Eh? (page 116), Elote (page 119), Peri Peri (page 122) and Butter Chicken (page 130).

POUTINE, EH?

Poutine is probably Canada's most famous dish and consists of fries, cheese curds and gravy. It originated in Quebec back in the 1950s. There is something magical about crispy fries and melted ooey-gooey cheese curds all swimming in a rich and comforting gravy. Throw some chicken wings on top and you've got a winning combo! Don't be afraid to get some sauce on your face. Napkins are a must.

SERVINGS: 4

2 lb (907 g) chicken wings, tips removed, drums and flats separated

2–3 medium-sized potatoes

½ cup (120 ml) Frank's RedHot Original or your favorite hot sauce

1½ cups (340 g) cheese curds, room temperature (or chunks of mozzarella)

SPICE RUB
1 tsp paprika

1 tsp garlic powder

1 tsp onion powder

¼ tsp chili powder

1 tsp brown sugar

Salt and pepper, to taste

POUTINE GRAVY SAUCE
3 tbsp (24 g) cornstarch

2 tbsp (30 ml) water

6 tbsp (84 g) unsalted butter

¼ cup (30 g) unbleached all-purpose flour

2½ cups (600 ml) beef broth

1¼ cup (300 ml) chicken broth

Salt and pepper, to taste

FOR SERVING
2 tbsp (12 g) chopped green onion

Leftover Poutine Gravy Sauce

Ranch dressing

With a paper towel, pat the wings dry. In a small bowl, combine all the ingredients for the spice rub. Sprinkle the prepared rub over the wings, coating evenly.

Prepare the fries. Cut the potatoes into ½-inch (1.3-cm) sticks. Cook them according to your preference, making sure to serve them warm with the wings.

Preheat the grill or smoker to 350°F (180°C), indirect heat.

Grill the wings for 40 minutes or until they reach a minimum internal temperature of 165°F (75°C), or 190°F (90°C) if you like them well done, flipping them halfway through the cooking time. To crisp the skin, move the wings to the direct heat side of the grill, turning occasionally, until the skin is dark golden or to your liking.

Meanwhile, prepare the gravy. In a small bowl, dissolve the cornstarch in the water and set aside. In a large saucepan over medium heat, melt the butter and add the flour. Cook, stirring regularly, for about 5 minutes, until the mixture turns golden brown. Add the beef and chicken broth and bring to a boil, stirring with a whisk. Stir in half the cornstarch mixture and simmer for 1 minute. If you like your gravy thicker, add more cornstarch mixture in small increments. Season to taste with salt and pepper. Keep warm.

Transfer the wings to a bowl and toss in the hot sauce. Place back on the grill grates for 5 to 10 minutes, or until the sauce settles. Place warm french fries on a plate and top with the wings, cheese curds, gravy and green onion. Serve them with leftover gravy and ranch dressing.

ELOTE

Elote is a classic Mexican street food that features corn on the cob charred on the grill, slathered in mayo and topped with tangy Cotija cheese, chili powder and fresh cilantro. This chicken wing recipe involves a similar process with all the classic tangy, bright and spicy flavors paired with a Cilantro Crema Dipping Sauce for a perfect finish!

SERVINGS: 4

2 lb (907 g) chicken wings, tips removed, drums and flats separated

1 tbsp (8 g) chili powder

½ tsp ground cumin

¼ tsp garlic powder

¼ tsp onion powder

¼ tsp ground coriander

¼ tsp kosher salt

¼ tsp cayenne pepper

⅛ tsp brown sugar

Juice of ½ lime

1 shucked ear of corn

CILANTRO CREMA DIPPING SAUCE

¼ cup (60 ml) mayonnaise

¼ cup (60 ml) sour cream

1 tbsp (8 g) chili powder

1 tbsp (8 g) garlic powder

1 tbsp (7 g) onion powder

1½ tbsp (21 ml) lime juice

2 tbsp (15 g) crumbled Cotija or feta cheese

2 tbsp (14 g) shredded mozzarella cheese

1 tbsp (1 g) chopped cilantro

FOR SERVING

2 tbsp (20 g) corn kernels (or grilled corn on the cob)

¼ cup (30 g) crumbled Cotija or feta cheese

1 tbsp (1 g) chopped cilantro

4 wedges lime

With a paper towel, pat the wings dry. In a small bowl, combine the chili powder, cumin, garlic powder, onion powder, ground coriander, salt, cayenne and brown sugar. In a medium bowl, toss the wings with the juice of half a lime and sprinkle the prepared rub over the wings, coating evenly. Alternatively, you can use Tajín® seasoning.

Preheat the grill or smoker to 350°F (180°C), indirect heat.

Grill the corn on the cob, turning occasionally, until charred on all sides, 10 to 15 minutes. Remove from the grill and let cool, about 5 minutes. Stand the corn cob upright and, holding the cob steady, use a sharp knife to make long downward strokes on the cob, separating the kernels from the cob.

Grill the wings for 40 minutes or until they reach a minimum internal temperature of 165°F (75°C), or 190°F (90°C) if you like them well done, flipping them halfway through the cooking time. To crisp the skin, move the wings to the direct heat side of the grill, turning occasionally, until the skin is dark golden or to your liking.

Meanwhile, prepare the dipping sauce. In a small bowl, combine the mayonnaise, sour cream, chili powder, garlic powder, onion powder, lime juice, Cotija, mozzarella cheese and cilantro.

Plate the wings and garnish them with 2 tablespoons (20 g) of corn kernels (or corn on the cob), Cotija, cilantro and lime wedges. Serve with the Cilantro Crema Dipping Sauce.

SWEET THAI CHILI

As you can probably tell from the name, sweet Thai chili sauce originated in Thailand and is one of the most popular condiment sauces in the cuisine. It is commonly made with Thai chili peppers or red jalapeños and is a thick sauce that is red or orange in color. These Sweet Thai Chili wings have a beautiful glistening glaze so get your sunglasses out. This recipe will stand out amongst the crowd, and you'll love how easy they are to make.

SERVINGS: 4

2 lb (907 g) chicken wings, tips removed, drums and flats separated

1 tsp garlic powder

1 tsp onion powder

1 tsp paprika

2 tsp (10 g) brown sugar

Salt and pepper, to taste

1 tbsp (15 ml) sesame oil

SWEET THAI CHILI SAUCE

1/3 cup (80 ml) plus 1 tbsp (15 ml) water, divided

2 tsp (5 g) cornstarch

1/3 cup (80 ml) rice vinegar

3 tbsp (45 ml) honey

2 cloves garlic, minced

1 tsp minced ginger

1 tbsp (15 ml) low-sodium soy sauce

2½ tsp (13 g) sambal oelek (chili paste)

1 tsp ketchup

FOR SERVING

Sesame seeds

2 tbsp (15 g) chopped peanuts

2 tbsp (12 g) chopped green onion

Leftover Sweet Thai Chili Sauce

With a paper towel, pat the wings dry. In a small bowl, combine the garlic powder, onion powder, paprika, brown sugar, salt and pepper. Toss the wings in the sesame oil and sprinkle the prepared rub over the wings, coating evenly.

Preheat the grill or smoker to 350°F (180°C), indirect heat.

Grill the wings for 40 minutes or until they reach a minimum internal temperature of 165°F (75°C), or 190°F (90°C) if you like them well done, flipping them halfway through the cooking time. To crisp the skin, move the wings to the direct heat side of the grill, turning occasionally, until the skin is dark golden or to your liking.

Meanwhile, prepare the sauce. In a small bowl, mix 1 tablespoon (15 ml) of water and the cornstarch into a smooth slurry. In a medium saucepan over medium heat, combine the rice vinegar, the remaining water, honey, garlic, ginger, soy sauce, sambal oelek and ketchup. Bring to a boil, stirring constantly. Add in the cornstarch mixture, stirring until thickened, about 1 minute.

Transfer the wings to a bowl and toss with Sweet Thai Chili Sauce until completely coated. Plate and garnish them with sesame seeds, peanuts and green onion. Serve them with the leftover sauce for dipping.

PERI PERI

Peri Peri (or Piri Piri) chicken is one of my all-time favorite Portuguese dishes. The sauce is traditionally made with African bird's eye chili, which is not always readily available, but I had to re-create these flavors in the form of chicken wings! They are spicy, garlicky, tangy and lemony for a bright and fresh finish. Impress your friends and family with this INSANELY delicious recipe.
Adjust the heat to your preference. Grab a *cerveja* (beer) and enjoy!

SERVINGS: 4

2 lb (907 g) chicken wings, tips removed, drums and flats separated

PERI PERI SAUCE
5 tbsp (75 ml) extra-virgin olive oil

3–4 tbsp (45–60 ml) freshly squeezed lemon juice

¼ cup (60 ml) apple cider vinegar

1 tbsp (5 g) cayenne pepper

1 tbsp (8 g) paprika

1–2 tbsp (9–17 g) minced garlic

2 tsp (5 g) salt

1 tsp black pepper

2 tbsp (10 g) crushed red pepper flakes

FOR SERVING
1 tbsp (4 g) chopped parsley

Lemon wedges

Leftover Peri Peri Sauce

With a paper towel, pat the wings dry. Place the wings in a shallow dish or resealable plastic bag. Prepare the sauce. In a food processor, place the olive oil, lemon juice, apple cider vinegar, cayenne, paprika, minced garlic, salt, pepper and crushed red pepper flakes. Blend until smooth. Pour enough of the marinade to cover the wings and toss to coat. Keep the rest aside. Cover and refrigerate for a minimum of 4 hours or overnight (the longer the better for best flavor results).

Preheat the grill or smoker to 350°F (180°C), indirect heat.

Grill the wings for 40 minutes or until they reach a minimum internal temperature of 165°F (75°C), or 190°F (90°C) if you like them well done, flipping them halfway through the cooking time. To crisp the skin, move the wings to the direct heat side of the grill, turning occasionally, until the skin is dark golden or to your liking. Baste the wings with the Peri Peri Sauce during the last 5 to 10 minutes.

Transfer the wings to a bowl and toss with the Peri Peri Sauce until completely coated. Plate the wings and garnish them with parsley. Serve them with lemon wedges and leftover sauce for dipping.

*See image on page 121 (shown on the bottom left).

SLAMMIN' SHAWARMA

These chicken wings are called "Slammin'" Shawarma for a reason. This recipe is a slam dunk! The marinade infuses the wings with mind-blowing Middle Eastern flavors for a tender, juicy and crispy finish leaving you wanting more. You'll be impressed after just one bite. My Garlic-Tahini Dipping Sauce provides an open court for a perfect slam dunk.

SERVINGS: 4

2 lb (907 g) chicken wings, tips removed, drums and flats separated

SHAWARMA MARINADE
2 tbsp (30 ml) extra-virgin olive oil
2 tsp (9 ml) freshly squeezed lemon juice
1 tsp honey
2 tsp (6 g) garlic powder
1 tsp onion powder
1 tsp coriander powder
1½ tsp (4 g) cumin powder
2 tsp (6 g) paprika
1 tsp turmeric powder
¼ tsp cayenne pepper
½ tsp ground cinnamon
⅛ tsp ground cloves
½ tsp ginger powder
Salt and pepper, to taste

GARLIC-TAHINI DIPPING SAUCE
2 cloves garlic, minced
2 tbsp (30 ml) lemon juice
¼ cup (60 ml) tahini paste
Pinch of cumin (optional)
4–8 tbsp (60–120 ml) water
Salt and pepper, to taste

FOR SERVING
1 tbsp (1 g) chopped cilantro
Garlic-Tahini Dipping Sauce

With a paper towel, pat the wings dry. Place the wings in a shallow dish or resealable plastic bag. Prepare the marinade. In a medium bowl, combine the olive oil, lemon juice, honey, garlic powder, onion powder, coriander powder, cumin, paprika, turmeric, cayenne pepper, ground cinnamon, ground cloves, ginger powder, salt and pepper. Pour the marinade over the wings and toss to coat. Cover and refrigerate for a minimum of 6 hours or preferably overnight (the longer the better for best flavor results). Remove the wings from the marinade and shake off any excess. Discard the marinade.

Preheat the grill or smoker to 350°F (180°C), indirect heat.

Grill the wings for 40 minutes or until they reach a minimum internal temperature of 165°F (75°C), or 190°F (90°C) if you like them well done, flipping them halfway through the cooking time. To crisp the skin, move the wings to the direct heat side of the grill, turning occasionally, until the skin is dark golden or to your liking.

Meanwhile, prepare the dipping sauce. In a small bowl, whisk together the garlic, lemon juice, tahini paste, cumin (if using), water, salt and pepper. Start with 2 tablespoons (30 ml) of water at a time, and add more if the sauce is too thick.

Plate the wings and garnish them with cilantro. Serve them with Garlic-Tahini Dipping Sauce.

*See image on page 121 (shown on the bottom right).

GREEK SOUVLAKI

Opa! These Greek Souvlaki–inspired chicken wings will make you want to smash plates on the ground with excitement! (I don't recommend doing so.) You'll be greeted with a beautifully browned and crispy skin with familiar souvlaki flavors. As if that isn't enough, my Tzatziki Dipping Sauce will round out the whole experience! Warm up some pita and place the wings on top to finish up any leftover dip.

SERVINGS: 4

2 lb (907 g) chicken wings, tips removed, drums and flats separated

12-inch (30-cm) bamboo skewers (optional)

MARINADE

¼ cup (60 ml) extra-virgin olive oil

1 tbsp (15 ml) freshly squeezed lemon juice

1 tbsp (15 ml) red wine vinegar

1 tbsp (5 g) dried oregano

1 tbsp (8 g) garlic powder

1 tsp paprika

Salt and pepper, to taste

TZATZIKI DIPPING SAUCE

¼ peeled and grated English cucumber

½ cup (120 ml) Greek yogurt

1 tsp extra-virgin olive oil

1 tsp freshly squeezed lemon juice

1 tsp white vinegar

2 tsp (2 g) finely chopped fresh dill

½ tbsp (4 g) minced garlic or more if you prefer a more garlicky flavor

Salt and pepper, to taste

FOR SERVING

2–3 pitas, warmed

2 tbsp (8 g) chopped parsley

2 tbsp (14 g) crumbled feta cheese

Kalamata olives

Tzatziki Dipping Sauce

With a paper towel, pat the wings dry and place them in a shallow dish. Prepare the marinade. In a medium bowl, whisk together the olive oil, lemon juice, red wine vinegar, oregano, garlic powder, paprika, salt and pepper. Pour the marinade over the wings and toss to coat. Cover and refrigerate for 1 to 8 hours (the longer the better).

Prepare the dipping sauce. Grate the cucumber and, working with one handful at a time, lightly squeeze it between your palms to remove excess moisture. Place it in a medium bowl. Add the yogurt, olive oil, lemon juice, white vinegar, dill, garlic, salt and pepper. Mix to combine. Cover and refrigerate until ready to serve.

Remove the wings from the marinade and shake off any excess. Discard the marinade. Skewer about five wings on each skewer, if using, and place them directly on the grill grates.

Preheat the grill or smoker to 350°F (180°C), indirect heat.

Grill the wings for 40 minutes or until they reach a minimum internal temperature of 165°F (75°C), or 190°F (90°C) if you like them well done, flipping them halfway through the cooking time. To crisp the skin, move the wings to the direct heat side of the grill, turning occasionally, until the skin is dark golden or to your liking.

Top the warmed pita with the wings and garnish them with parsley, feta and olives. Serve them with Tzatziki Dipping Sauce.

ITALIAN BRUSCHETTA

I've taken one of my all-time favorite comfort food classic appetizers and created a chicken wing recipe. They are bursting with flavor, tender, juicy, cheesy and topped with a bruschetta mixture and balsamic glaze drizzle that take these wings to the next level. I love these for get-togethers or a weeknight meal.

SERVINGS: 4

NOTE: If you decide to skip the mozzarella cheese, simply top the wings with the bruschetta mixture, balsamic glaze and garnish once they're fully cooked.

2 lb (907 g) chicken wings, tips removed, drums and flats separated

¾ cup (84 g) shredded mozzarella cheese (optional, see Note)

MARINADE

2 tbsp (30 ml) extra-virgin olive oil

1 tbsp (15 ml) balsamic vinegar

2 tsp (6 g) Italian seasoning

1 tsp paprika

2 cloves garlic, minced

1 tsp onion powder

Salt and pepper, to taste

BALSAMIC GLAZE SAUCE

½ cup (120 ml) balsamic vinegar

3 tbsp (45 ml) honey

ITALIAN BRUSCHETTA TOPPING

3–4 finely chopped Roma tomatoes

1½ tbsp (21 g) extra-virgin olive oil

2 tsp (6 g) minced garlic

½ tsp oregano

Salt and pepper, to taste

FOR SERVING

Italian Bruschetta Topping

Balsamic Glaze Sauce

¼ cup (25 g) grated Parmesan cheese

4 tbsp (10 g) fresh chopped basil

Crushed red pepper flakes (optional)

Ranch dressing

With a paper towel, pat the wings dry. Next, prepare the marinade by whisking together the olive oil, balsamic vinegar, Italian seasoning, paprika, garlic, onion powder, salt and pepper. Marinate the wings in the refrigerator for 2 hours or overnight (the longer the better).

Make the sauce. In a small saucepan over medium-high heat, whisk together the balsamic vinegar and honey. Once it begins to bubble, reduce the heat and simmer for 5 to 10 minutes, until reduced by half. Let cool.

Preheat the grill or smoker to 350°F (180°C), indirect heat.

Grill the wings for 40 minutes or until they reach a minimum internal temperature of 165°F (75°C), or 190°F (90°C) if you like them well done, flipping them halfway through. To crisp the skin, move the wings to the direct heat side of the grill, turning occasionally, until the skin is dark golden.

Meanwhile, prepare the bruschetta. In a medium bowl, combine the tomatoes, olive oil, garlic, oregano, salt and pepper.

Turn the grill up to 400°F (200°C). Place the wings on a lined baking tray. Top with mozzarella cheese, if desired. Place them back on the grill for 5 to 10 minutes or until the cheese melts.

Plate the wings and top with the bruschetta, glaze sauce, Parmesan cheese, basil and red pepper flakes (if using). Serve with ranch dressing.

KOREAN BBQ

These wings hit all the right flavor notes. They are sweet, savory, spicy and will disappear as fast as they hit the grill. Be sure to grab a few before putting them out—it's okay, I won't tell. This sauce is a game changer that will make you a hero at any party, thanks to the Korean pepper paste gochujang, which adds to the scrumptious flavor of these wings.

SERVINGS: 4

2 lb (907 g) chicken wings, tips removed, drums and flats separated

1 tsp garlic powder

½ tsp onion powder

1 tsp ginger powder

1 tsp paprika

1 tsp salt

½ tsp black pepper

1 tsp brown sugar

1 tbsp (15 ml) sesame oil

KOREAN BBQ SAUCE

2 tbsp (28 g) unsalted butter

½ cup (120 ml) low-sodium soy sauce

2 tbsp (30 ml) water

¼ cup (60 ml) gochujang paste or sriracha

2 tbsp (30 ml) honey

1 tbsp (14 g) brown sugar (optional)

1 tbsp (8 g) minced garlic

1 tbsp (6 g) minced ginger

1½ tbsp (22 ml) rice wine vinegar

FOR SERVING

Sesame seeds

2 tbsp (12 g) chopped green onion

Leftover Korean BBQ Sauce

With a paper towel, pat the wings dry. In a small bowl, combine the garlic powder, onion powder, ginger powder, paprika, salt, pepper and brown sugar. Toss the wings in the sesame oil and sprinkle the prepared rub over the wings, coating evenly.

Preheat the grill or smoker to 350°F (180°C), indirect heat.

Grill the wings for 40 minutes or until they reach a minimum internal temperature of 165°F (75°C), or 190°F (90°C) if you like them well done, flipping them halfway through the cooking time. To crisp the skin, move the wings to the direct heat side of the grill, turning occasionally, until the skin is dark golden or to your liking.

Meanwhile, prepare the sauce. In a medium saucepan over medium-high heat, melt the butter and combine the soy sauce, water, gochujang, honey, brown sugar (if using), garlic, ginger and rice wine vinegar. Bring to a boil, stirring constantly. Reduce the heat to low and simmer for about 5 minutes or until the sauce has slightly thickened.

Transfer the wings to a bowl and toss with the Korean BBQ Sauce until completely coated. Plate and garnish them with sesame seeds and green onion. Serve them with leftover sauce for dipping.

BUTTER CHICKEN

What's your favorite Indian take-out dish? Mine is butter chicken! I love the rich and creamy aromatic flavors of this sauce that's complimented by the flavor-infused wing marinade. This chicken wing recipe is one of the best you'll ever make. Combining these layers of flavor to create mind-blowing wings just makes sense. Try it, you'll love it!

SERVINGS: 4

2 lb (907 g) chicken wings, tips removed, drums and flats separated

MARINADE
2 tsp (6 g) garam masala
1 tsp cumin
1 tsp turmeric powder
½ tsp chili powder
½ tsp cayenne pepper
½ tsp coriander
½ tsp paprika
1 tsp salt
2 cloves garlic, minced
1 tbsp (6 g) minced ginger

BUTTER CHICKEN SAUCE
2 tbsp (28 g) butter
2 cloves garlic, minced
1 tbsp (6 g) minced ginger
1 tbsp (11 g) onion powder
2 tsp (6 g) garam masala
1 tsp cumin
½ tsp coriander
½ tsp chili powder
1 tsp brown sugar (optional)
1½ cups (360 ml) tomato passata (tomato puree)
1 cup (240 ml) heavy cream

FOR SERVING
1 tbsp (1 g) chopped cilantro
Leftover Butter Chicken Sauce

With a paper towel, pat the wings dry. Prepare the marinade. In a small bowl, combine the garam masala, cumin, turmeric, chili powder, cayenne, coriander, paprika and salt. Place the wings in a resealable bag or shallow dish. Top the wings with the garlic, ginger and the combined seasoning; toss to coat. Cover and refrigerate for 3 to 24 hours (the longer the better for best flavor results).

Preheat the grill or smoker to 350°F (180°C), indirect heat.

Grill the wings for 40 minutes or until they reach a minimum internal temperature of 165°F (75°C), or 190°F (90°C) if you like them well done, flipping them halfway through the cooking time. To crisp the skin, move the wings to the direct heat side of the grill, turning occasionally, until the skin is dark golden or to your liking.

Meanwhile, prepare the sauce. In a large saucepan over medium heat, melt the butter. Add the garlic and ginger, and sauté for 1 to 2 minutes, until fragrant. Next, add the onion powder, garam masala, cumin, coriander, chili powder and brown sugar (if using). Cook for about 15 seconds and add the tomato puree. Continue cooking for 10 to 15 minutes and stir in the cream. Simmer for an additional 5 to 8 minutes or until the sauce is thick and bubbling.

Transfer the wings to a bowl and toss with the Butter Chicken Sauce until completely coated. Plate the wings and garnish them with cilantro. Serve them with leftover sauce for dipping.

JAMAICAN JERK

I first fell in love with jerk chicken at the Toronto (Canada) Caribbean Caribana Festival, which is North America's largest cultural festival dating back to 1967. It was once a three-day event that has since grown into three weeks of celebration, diffusing into most of the city with its infectious feel-good vibes. These Jamaican Jerk wings will give you those vibes. The aroma alone is intoxicating. They are spicy, full of flavor and the perfect snack.

SERVINGS: 4

JERK MARINADE

1 tbsp (6 g) ground allspice
½ tsp cayenne pepper
1½ tsp (1 g) ground sage
¾ tsp ground cinnamon
¾ tsp ground nutmeg
2 tbsp (17 g) chili powder
½ tsp cumin
2 tbsp (14 g) onion powder
2 tbsp (17 g) garlic powder
1 tbsp (8 g) paprika
½ tsp ginger powder
1 tbsp (3 g) dried thyme
¾ cup (120 g) chopped white onion
1–2 Scotch bonnet pepper, seeded and chopped
¾ cup (180 ml) white vinegar
½ cup (120 ml) pulp-free orange juice
¼ cup (60 ml) extra-virgin olive oil
¼ cup (60 ml) low-sodium soy sauce
2 tbsp (30 ml) freshly squeezed lime juice
1 tbsp (15 ml) freshly squeezed lemon juice
1 tbsp (8 g) black pepper
1 tsp salt

2 lb (907 g) chicken wings, tips removed, drums and flats separated

FOR SERVING

2 tbsp (12 g) chopped green onion
Lime wedges

In a blender or food processor, make the Jerk Marinade by blending the allspice, cayenne pepper, sage, cinnamon, nutmeg, chili powder, cumin, onion powder, garlic powder, paprika, ginger powder, thyme, onion, Scotch bonnet pepper, vinegar, orange juice, olive oil, soy sauce, lime and lemon juices, pepper and salt. Puree until smooth.

With a paper towel, pat the wings dry. Place the wings in a shallow dish or resealable plastic bag, pour the marinade over them and toss to coat. Cover and refrigerate for at least 8 hours, preferably overnight, if possible. Remove the wings from the marinade and shake off any excess. Discard the marinade.

Preheat the grill or smoker to 350°F (180°C), indirect heat.

Grill the wings for 40 minutes or until they reach a minimum internal temperature of 165°F (75°C), or 190°F (90°C) if you like them well done, flipping them halfway through the cooking time. To crisp the skin, move the wings to the direct heat side of the grill, turning occasionally, until the skin is dark golden or to your liking.

Plate the wings and garnish them with green onion. Serve them with lime wedges.

ORANGE CHICKEN

Everyone has a guilty pleasure when it comes to take-out. If orange chicken is one of yours, then you must make these wings! They are simple to make and the tantalizing sticky coating of sweet and citrus orange flavors of the sauce will have you wishing you made more.

SERVINGS: 4

2 lb (907 g) chicken wings, tips removed, drums and flats separated

ORANGE CHICKEN MARINADE

½ cup (120 ml) freshly squeezed orange juice

1 tbsp (6 g) orange zest

¼ cup (60 ml) low-sodium soy sauce

1 tbsp (15 ml) white vinegar

2 cloves garlic, minced

1 tsp sriracha

¼ tsp ground ginger

1 tsp onion powder

2 tbsp (28 g) brown sugar

Salt and pepper, to taste

ORANGE CHICKEN SAUCE

1 tbsp (15 ml) sesame oil

2 cloves garlic, minced

1 tsp minced ginger

1 cup (240 ml) orange juice

2 tbsp (30 ml) rice wine vinegar

2 tbsp (30 ml) low-sodium soy sauce

¼ cup (55 g) brown sugar

½ tsp crushed red pepper flakes

1 tbsp (8 g) cornstarch

2 tbsp (30 ml) water

Zest from 1 orange

FOR SERVING

Sesame seeds

2 tbsp (12 g) chopped green onion

Orange zest

Leftover Orange Chicken Sauce

Ranch dressing (optional)

With a paper towel, pat the wings dry. Place the wings in a shallow dish or resealable plastic bag. Prepare the marinade. In a medium bowl, whisk together the orange juice, orange zest, soy sauce, white vinegar, garlic, sriracha, ground ginger, onion powder, brown sugar, salt and pepper. Pour the marinade over the wings and toss to coat. Cover and refrigerate for at least 2 hours (the longer the better for best flavor results). Remove the wings from the marinade and shake off any excess. Discard the marinade.

Preheat the grill or smoker to 350°F (180°C), indirect heat.

Grill the wings for 40 minutes or until they reach a minimum internal temperature of 165°F (75°C), or 190°F (90°C) if you like them well done, flipping them halfway through the cooking time. To crisp the skin, move the wings to the direct heat side of the grill, turning occasionally, until the skin is dark golden or to your liking.

Meanwhile, prepare the sauce. In a medium saucepan over medium heat, add the sesame oil, minced garlic and minced ginger. Stir frequently and sauté until the garlic and ginger start to brown, 2 to 3 minutes. Whisk in the orange juice, rice vinegar, soy sauce, brown sugar and crushed red pepper flakes. Continue cooking for about 3 minutes or until the brown sugar has dissolved. In a small bowl, whisk together the cornstarch and water until a smooth slurry forms and add it to the mixture. Stir frequently and cook for about 10 minutes or until the mixture starts to thicken. Remove from the heat and add the orange zest.

Transfer the wings to a bowl and toss with the Orange Chicken Sauce until completely coated. Plate the wings and garnish them with sesame seeds, green onion and orange zest. Serve them with leftover sauce and/or ranch dressing.

*See image on page 132 (shown on the top right).

AL PASTOR

Al pastor tacos are an incredibly tasty Mexican dish that uses thin slices of pork marinated in a sweet and tangy pineapple-based sauce with traditional flavors. I had to incorporate these flavors into chicken wings and WOW they are INCREDIBLY delicious! Taco Tuesday and Wing Crush Wednesday collide to create a beautiful explosion of flavor. These wings come to the rescue when you can't decide whether you want tacos or wings.

SERVINGS: 4

AL PASTOR MARINADE
2 cups (480 ml) water
4 dried guajillo chiles, de-seeded
1 dried ancho chile, de-seeded
½ cup (120 ml) orange juice
½ cup (120 ml) pineapple juice
1 tsp garlic powder
1 tsp onion powder
1 tsp paprika
1 tsp oregano
1 tsp cumin
⅛ tsp cayenne pepper
1 tsp brown sugar
2 chipotle peppers in adobo sauce
2 tsp (10 ml) adobo sauce (from canned chipotle peppers)
Salt and pepper, to taste

2 lb (907 g) chicken wings, tips removed, drums and flats separated

PINEAPPLE-JALAPEÑO DIPPING SAUCE
2 pineapple rounds, peeled, cored and cut into ½-inch (1.3-cm) slices
1 fresh jalapeño
1 clove garlic
Juice of 1 lime
¼ cup (60 ml) mayonnaise
2 tbsp (2 g) chopped cilantro
Salt and pepper, to taste

FOR SERVING
1 tbsp (1 g) chopped cilantro
Lime wedges
Pineapple-Jalapeño Dipping Sauce

Prepare the marinade. In a medium pot over medium heat, add the water, guajillo chiles and ancho chile. Bring to a boil and cook on low for about 15 minutes. Let cool.

In a food processor or blender, place the guajillo chiles, ancho chile, orange juice, pineapple juice, garlic powder, onion powder, paprika, oregano, cumin, cayenne, brown sugar, chipotles in adobo, adobo sauce, salt and pepper. Blend until everything is completely combined and smooth. Add some reserved chili water if the marinade is too thick. Strain the marinade over a bowl.

With a paper towel, pat the wings dry. Place the wings in a shallow dish or resealable plastic bag and pour in enough marinade to cover. Keep any excess aside to baste the wings. Toss to coat. Cover and refrigerate for 4 hours or overnight (the longer the better for best flavor results). Shake off any excess and discard the marinade.

Preheat the grill or smoker to 350°F (180°C), indirect heat.

Grill the pineapple rounds and jalapeño, turning occasionally, until charred on all sides, 10 to 15 minutes.

Grill the wings for 40 minutes or until they reach a minimum internal temperature of 165°F (75°C), or 190°F (90°C) if you like them well done, flipping them halfway through the cooking time. To crisp the skin, move the wings to the direct heat side of the grill, turning occasionally, until the skin is dark golden or to your liking. Baste the wings with the leftover unused Al Pastor Marinade during the last 5 to 10 minutes.

Meanwhile, prepare the dipping sauce. Place the pineapple rounds, jalapeño (stem removed), garlic and lime juice into a blender. Puree until smooth. Transfer into a small bowl and combine with the mayonnaise, cilantro, salt and pepper.

Plate the wings and garnish them with cilantro. Serve them with lime wedges and the Pineapple-Jalapeño Dipping Sauce.

*See image on page 132 (shown on the bottom).

SPICY CURRY

There are a variety of curry dishes that use a combination of spices like turmeric powder, cumin, coriander and ginger that are often used in Indian cooking. Chicken curry is one of the most popular dishes and you'll understand why after just one bite. These chicken wings are full of flavor and finished off in a slightly spicy, rich and creamy curry sauce.

SERVINGS: 4

2 lb (907 g) chicken wings, tips removed, drums and flats separated

MARINADE
2 tsp (5 g) yellow curry powder
1 tsp cumin
1 tsp turmeric powder
½ tsp chili powder
½ tsp cayenne pepper
½ tsp coriander
½ tsp paprika
1 tsp salt, or to taste
1 tsp fish sauce (oyster sauce)
2 cloves garlic, minced
1 tbsp (6 g) minced ginger

SPICY CURRY SAUCE
1½ tbsp (22 ml) vegetable oil
2 cloves garlic, minced
2 tsp (4 g) minced ginger
2 tbsp (14 g) yellow curry powder
1 tbsp (7 g) onion powder
2 tsp (5 g) garam masala
½ tsp coriander
1 tsp cayenne pepper, or to taste
½ cup (120 ml) full-fat coconut milk or heavy cream
1 tsp tomato paste
1½ cups (360 ml) low-sodium chicken stock
1 tsp brown sugar (optional)
Salt, to taste

FOR SERVING
1 tbsp (1 g) chopped cilantro
Leftover Spicy Curry Sauce

With a paper towel, pat the wings dry. Prepare the marinade. In a small bowl, combine the curry powder, cumin, turmeric, chili powder, cayenne, coriander, paprika and salt. Place the wings in a shallow dish and top them with the fish sauce, garlic, ginger and combined seasonings; toss to coat. Cover and refrigerate for 3 to 24 hours (the longer the better).

Preheat the grill or smoker to 350°F (180°C), indirect heat. Grill the wings for 40 minutes or until they reach a minimum internal temperature of 165°F (75°C), or 190°F (90°C) if you like them well done, flipping them halfway through. To crisp the skin, move the wings to the direct heat side of the grill, turning occasionally, until the skin is dark golden.

Meanwhile, prepare the sauce. In a large saucepan over medium-low heat, heat the oil and add the garlic and ginger. Sauté for 1 to 2 minutes until fragrant. Next, add the curry powder, onion powder, garam masala, coriander and cayenne. Cook for 15 seconds and add the coconut milk and tomato paste. Continue cooking for 15 to 20 minutes and stir in the chicken stock and brown sugar (if using). Depending on the consistency you want, either remove from the heat or simmer for 5 to 8 minutes until the sauce is thick and bubbling. Taste and add salt as desired.

Transfer the wings to a bowl and toss with the Spicy Curry Sauce until completely coated. Plate the wings and garnish them with cilantro. Serve them with leftover sauce for dipping.

ASIAN STING

These chicken wings will sting—in the best possible way. They are hot and sticky, but the heat level can be easily adjusted to your preference. Pair them with your favorite beer or rosé wine to cool your palate. This sauce is so incredible, you will want to double it. To do so, simply double the ingredients.

SERVINGS: 4

2 lb (907 g) chicken wings, tips removed, drums and flats separated
1 tsp garlic powder
1 tsp onion powder
1 tsp paprika
1 tsp brown sugar
½ tsp cayenne pepper
Salt and pepper, to taste
1 tsp cornstarch

ASIAN STING SAUCE
2 tbsp (30 ml) sesame oil
2 cloves garlic, minced
½ tsp minced ginger

½ tsp crushed red pepper flakes
1 tbsp (15 ml) low-sodium soy sauce
1½ tbsp (22 ml) sriracha
2 tbsp (30 ml) mirin
2 tbsp (30 ml) rice vinegar
2 tbsp (30 ml) honey

FOR SERVING
Sesame seeds
2 tbsp (12 g) chopped green onion
¼ tsp crushed red pepper flakes
Leftover Asian Sting Sauce
Ranch dressing (optional)

With a paper towel, pat the wings dry. In a small bowl, combine the garlic powder, onion powder, paprika, brown sugar, cayenne, salt, pepper and cornstarch. Sprinkle the prepared rub over the wings, coating evenly.

Preheat the grill or smoker to 350°F (180°C), indirect heat.

Grill the wings for 40 minutes or until they reach a minimum internal temperature of 165°F (75°C), or 190°F (90°C) if you like them well done, flipping them halfway through the cooking time. To crisp the skin, move the wings to the direct heat side of the grill, turning occasionally, until the skin is dark golden or to your liking.

Meanwhile, prepare the sauce. In a small saucepan over low heat, add the sesame oil, minced garlic, minced ginger and crushed red pepper flakes. Let the flavors slowly infuse the oil for 10 to 15 minutes or until the garlic and ginger start to brown, stirring occasionally.

In a small bowl, whisk to combine the soy sauce, sriracha, mirin, rice vinegar and honey. Pour the mixture into the saucepan and increase the heat to high. Bring to a boil, stirring frequently for 1 to 2 minutes.

Transfer the wings to a bowl and toss with the Asian Sting Sauce until completely coated. Plate the wings and garnish them with sesame seeds, green onion and crushed red pepper flakes. Serve them with leftover sauce and/or ranch dressing.

*See image on page 139 (shown on the bottom).

GENERAL TSO

General Tso chicken is one of my favorite take-out dishes. I was first introduced to this mouthwatering sweet, sticky and spicy dish over a decade ago at a Chinese restaurant in downtown Toronto. These chicken wings have all those familiar flavors. You'll be hooked, and once your friends and family try them, they'll be saying: "These are tso delicious!" Keep the napkins handy. Adjust the heat to your preference.

SERVINGS: 4

2 lb (907 g) chicken wings, tips removed, drums and flats separated

1 tsp garlic powder

1 tsp onion powder

2 tsp (6 g) paprika

2 tsp (10 g) brown sugar

½ tsp ginger powder

¼ tsp cayenne pepper

1 tsp cornstarch

Salt and pepper, to taste

1 tbsp (15 ml) sesame oil

GENERAL TSO SAUCE

3 tbsp (45 ml) sesame oil

1 tbsp (8 g) minced garlic

1 tbsp (6 g) minced ginger

1 tsp crushed red pepper flakes

2 tbsp (30 ml) low-sodium soy sauce

2 tbsp (30 ml) rice vinegar

1 tsp paprika

3 tbsp (45 ml) honey

1 tbsp (15 ml) water

1 tsp sesame seeds

FOR SERVING

Sesame seeds

2 tbsp (12 g) chopped green onion

Ranch or blue cheese dressing (optional)

With a paper towel, pat the wings dry. In a small bowl, combine the garlic powder, onion powder, paprika, brown sugar, ginger powder, cayenne, cornstarch, salt and pepper. Toss the wings in the sesame oil and sprinkle the prepared rub over the wings, coating evenly.

Preheat the grill or smoker to 350°F (180°C), indirect heat.

Grill the wings for 40 minutes or until they reach a minimum internal temperature of 165°F (75°C), or 190°F (90°C) if you like them well done, flipping them halfway through the cooking time. To crisp the skin, move the wings to the direct heat side of the grill, turning occasionally, until the skin is dark golden or to your liking.

Meanwhile, prepare the sauce. In a small saucepan over medium heat, heat the sesame oil and add the minced garlic and minced ginger. Stir frequently and sauté until the garlic and ginger are fragrant and start to brown, 2 to 3 minutes. Stir in the crushed red pepper flakes, soy sauce, rice vinegar, paprika, honey, water and sesame seeds. Stir frequently and bring to a boil, then reduce the heat to a simmer. Simmer for about 5 minutes or until the sauce is thickened.

Transfer the wings to a bowl and toss with the General Tso Sauce until completely coated. Plate the wings and garnish them with sesame seeds and green onion. Serve them with the leftover sauce and/or ranch dressing.

*See image on page 139 (shown on the top left).

CUBAN MOJO

These Cuban Mojo chicken wings are infused with a marinade made with citrus, garlic and spices resulting in tender and juicy wings. Every bite is full of flavor. These are the ultimate summer recipe! Your friends and family will be raving about how flavorful they are. Serve them with my Cilantro Crema Dipping Sauce for the perfect finish.

SERVINGS: 4

CUBAN MOJO MARINADE
1/3 cup (80 ml) freshly squeezed orange juice
Zest of 1 orange
1/4 cup (60 ml) freshly squeezed lime juice
Zest of 1 lime
1/2 cup (120 ml) extra-virgin olive oil
1 tsp ground cumin
1 tsp oregano
4 cloves garlic
1 tsp onion powder
1/4 tsp cayenne pepper
1/4 cup (4 g) fresh cilantro
Salt and pepper, to taste

2 lb (907 g) chicken wings, tips removed, drums and flats separated

2 tbsp (19 g) granulated garlic
1 tbsp (7 g) onion powder
1 tbsp (18 g) salt
1/2 tbsp (4 g) black pepper
1/2 tbsp (4 g) turmeric
1 tbsp (5 g) oregano

CILANTRO CREMA DIPPING SAUCE
1/4 cup (60 ml) mayonnaise
1/4 cup (60 ml) sour cream
1 tbsp (8 g) chili powder
1 tbsp (8 g) garlic powder
1 tbsp (7 g) onion powder
1 1/2 tbsp (22 ml) lime juice
1 tbsp (1 g) chopped cilantro

FOR SERVING
1 tbsp (1 g) chopped cilantro
Lime wedges
Cilantro Crema Dipping Sauce

Prepare the marinade. In a blender or food processor, place the orange juice, orange zest, lime juice, lime zest, olive oil, cumin, oregano, garlic, onion powder, cayenne, fresh cilantro, salt and pepper. Process for about 10 seconds only; you don't want the sauce to become too creamy.

With a paper towel, pat the wings dry. Place the wings in a shallow dish or resealable plastic bag and pour in the marinade. Toss to coat. Cover and refrigerate for 4 hours or overnight (the longer the better). Remove the wings and discard the marinade. In a small bowl, combine the granulated garlic, onion powder, salt, black pepper, turmeric and oregano. Sprinkle the rub over the wings, coating evenly.

Preheat the grill or smoker to 350°F (180°C), indirect heat.

Grill the wings for 40 minutes or until they reach a minimum internal temperature of 165°F (75°C), or 190°F (90°C) if you like them well done, flipping them halfway through. To crisp the skin, move the wings to the direct heat side of the grill, turning occasionally, until the skin is golden.

Meanwhile, prepare the dipping sauce. In a small bowl, combine all the ingredients.

Plate the wings and garnish them with cilantro. Serve them with lime wedges and the Cilantro Crema Dipping Sauce.

HULI HULI (TROPICAL HAWAIIAN WINGS)

2 lb (907 g) chicken wings, tips removed, drums and flats separated

Salt and pepper, to taste

HULI HULI MARINADE AND SAUCE

1 cup (240 ml) pineapple juice, unsweetened

¼ cup (60 ml) low sodium soy sauce

¼ cup (55 g) brown sugar

¼ cup (60 ml) ketchup

¼ cup (60 ml) low sodium chicken stock

1 tbsp (15 ml) sriracha

3 cloves garlic, minced

2 tsp (4 g) freshly grated ginger

FOR SERVING

1 pineapple, cut into wedges

1 thinly sliced green onion

Leftover sauce

You'll be feeling the tropical vibes that the pineapple juice and ginger bring through to these sweet, tangy and bright hot teriyaki-like chicken wings. This recipe is ALL about the sauce. *Huli huli* means "turn turn"—huli huli chicken is a local specialty, where vendors thread chickens on a special rotating grill and grill them over charcoal. Make sure to turn the wings often so that they crisp evenly.

SERVINGS: 4

With a paper towel, pat the wings dry. Place the wings in a shallow dish or resealable plastic bag. Prepare the marinade. In a medium bowl, whisk together the pineapple juice, soy sauce, brown sugar, ketchup, chicken stock, sriracha, garlic and ginger. Pour enough sauce to cover the wings and toss to coat. Cover and refrigerate for 1 to 8 hours (the longer the better for best flavor results). Keep the remaining sauce in a bowl covered with plastic wrap and refrigerate.

Remove the wings from the marinade and season with salt and pepper. Discard the used marinade.

Preheat the grill or smoker to 350°F (180°C), indirect heat.

Grill the pineapple wedges, turning occasionally, until charred on all sides, 10 to 15 minutes.

Grill the wings for 40 minutes or until they reach a minimum internal temperature of 165°F (74°C), or 190°F (90°C) if you like them well done. To crisp the skin, move the wings to the direct heat side of the grill, turning occasionally, until the skin is dark golden or to your liking.

Meanwhile, pour the reserved marinade into a saucepan and bring to a boil over medium-high heat. Reduce the heat to low and simmer for 10 to 12 minutes, or until the sauce thickens.

Transfer the wings to a bowl and toss with the thickened sauce until completely coated. Place the wings back on the grill grates for 5 to 10 minutes, until the sauce settles, or serve immediately. Plate the wings and garnish them with green onion.

Serve them with the grilled pineapple and leftover sauce.

KUNG PAO

These Kung Pao chicken wings have the perfect combination of sweet, spicy and salty flavors, making them the perfect fusion food. They're topped with roasted peanuts and tossed in a delicious thick sauce that will make these one of your most requested recipes.

SERVINGS: 4

2 lb (907 g) chicken wings, tips removed, drums and flats separated

MARINADE

1½ tbsp (22 ml) low-sodium soy sauce

1 tbsp (15 ml) Shaoxing wine or dry sherry

¼ tsp sesame oil

1 tbsp (8 g) garlic powder

2 tsp (4 g) ginger powder

½ tsp cayenne powder

2 tsp (5 g) cornstarch

⅛ tsp white pepper, or to taste

KUNG PAO SAUCE

½ cup (120 ml) chicken stock or water

1 tsp cornstarch

1 tsp vegetable oil

1 tsp minced ginger

1 clove garlic, minced

8 to 10 whole dried red chili peppers, or to taste

½ tsp crushed red pepper flakes

1 tsp Shaoxing wine or dry sherry

1 tbsp (15 ml) Chinese black vinegar or balsamic vinegar

½ tsp sesame oil

2 tbsp (28 g) brown sugar, or to taste

2 tsp (10 ml) rice vinegar

1 tsp hoisin sauce

1 tsp light soy sauce

¼ tsp dark soy sauce

FOR SERVING

Sesame seeds

Unsalted roasted and chopped peanuts

2 tbsp (12 g) chopped green onion

Leftover Kung Pao Sauce

With a paper towel, pat the wings dry. Place the wings in a large mixing bowl. Prepare the marinade. In a medium bowl, whisk together the soy sauce, Shaoxing wine, sesame oil, garlic powder, ginger powder, cayenne, cornstarch and white pepper. Pour the marinade over the wings and toss to coat. Set aside for 15 to 20 minutes.

Preheat the grill or smoker to 350°F (180°C), indirect heat.

Grill the wings for 40 minutes or until they reach a minimum internal temperature of 165°F (75°C), or 190°F (90°C) if you like them well done, flipping them halfway through the cooking time. To crisp the skin, move the wings to the direct heat side of the grill, turning occasionally, until the skin is dark golden or to your liking.

Meanwhile, prepare the sauce. In a small bowl, mix the chicken stock or water and cornstarch into a smooth slurry. In a medium saucepan over medium heat, add the vegetable oil, ginger and garlic. Stir frequently and sauté until the garlic and ginger start to brown, 2 to 3 minutes. Add the dried red chili peppers and crushed red pepper flakes. Sauté for about 10 seconds and stir in the Shaoxing wine, Chinese black vinegar, sesame oil, brown sugar, rice vinegar, hoisin sauce, light soy sauce and dark soy sauce. Stir frequently and bring to a simmer. Stir in the chicken stock/cornstarch slurry and simmer for about 5 minutes or until the sauce is thickened.

Transfer the wings to a bowl and toss with the Kung Pao Sauce until completely coated. Plate and garnish them with sesame seeds, peanuts and green onion. Serve the wings with leftover sauce for dipping.

*See image on page 114.

WINGS GONE WILD

It's about to get wild over here! This chapter has some of the most outrageous and innovative pairings that will satisfy any palate. These chicken wing flavors will change your life. The recipes will be an instant hit at any gathering, from Peanut Butter and Jelly (page 165), Strawberry Cheesecake (page 166), French Toast (page 160), Jalapeño Popper Stuffed (page 150), Chicken and Waffle (page 162) and many more. Take a walk on the wild side.

JALAPEÑO POPPER STUFFED

These chicken wings want to be jalapeño mouth. Jalapeño poppers are one of the most popular game day appetizers along with chicken wings. Why not combine the two for an explosion of flavor? These are epic and anyone that has tried them has been blown away. The creamy, cheesy, spicy and bacon-filled stuffing just hits different after that first bite, and my Chipotle Dipping Sauce really puts them over the top. Grab a beer and enjoy!

SERVINGS: 4

JALAPEÑO POPPER STUFFING

8 to 10 strips thinly cut bacon, chopped into small pieces

2 diced fresh jalapeños, seeds and flesh removed

8 oz (240 g) cream cheese, room temperature

1 cup (112 g) shredded cheddar cheese

2 lb (907 g) chicken wings, tips removed, drums and flats separated

Your favorite BBQ rub (I use Reload Rub & Seasoning Co.™ Double Action)

CHIPOTLE DIPPING SAUCE

½ cup (120 ml) mayonnaise

¼ cup (60 ml) sour cream

1–2 tbsp (15–30 ml) adobo sauce (from canned chipotle peppers)

1 tsp garlic powder

1–2 tsp (5–10 ml) freshly squeezed lime juice

Salt, to taste

FOR SERVING

2 tbsp (12 g) chopped green onion

Prepare the stuffing. In a medium saucepan over medium heat, fry the bacon for 5 to 7 minutes, or until crispy, and add the chopped jalapeños. Sauté until fragrant and translucent, 2 to 3 minutes. Strain the grease. In a large bowl, combine the cream cheese, cheddar cheese, bacon and jalapeños. Place the mixture into a piping bag or stuff the wings by hand.

With a paper towel, pat the wings dry. Stuff the wings by loosening the skin around the drumette and flat areas (on the meatier side opposite of the bone) with your fingers/thumb to create a pocket that can be stuffed. Fill each wing with about ½ teaspoon of the Jalapeño Popper Stuffing. Push the stuffing as far down as possible. Do not overstuff, and leave some room to close the flap.

Sprinkle your favorite rub over the wings, coating evenly.

Preheat the grill or smoker to 350°F (180°C), indirect heat. Place the wings, stuffing side up, on the grill grates.

Grill the wings for 40 minutes or until they reach a minimum internal temperature of 165°F (75°C), or 190°F (90°C) if you like them well done. Flipping the wings is not recommended. Some filling will come out during the grilling process, which is not unusual.

Prepare the dipping sauce. In a small bowl, whisk together the mayonnaise, sour cream, adobo sauce, garlic powder, lime juice and salt.

Plate the wings and garnish them with green onion. Serve them with the Chipotle Dipping Sauce.

MAC 'N' CHEESE STUFFED

I now pronounce you Mac 'n' Wing. These chicken wings are a match made in clucking heaven. Mac 'n' cheese is one of the most popular BBQ side dishes and wings, well … who doesn't love them? This is one of my favorite mash-ups. I highly recommend making these for game day, a party or when you're simply craving something INSANELY delicious. This recipe never disappoints and is always a crowd-pleaser. These wings will be the talk of the week.

SERVINGS: 4

1½ cups (372 g) leftover mac 'n' cheese or freshly made

2 lb (907 g) chicken wings, tips removed, drums and flats separated

1 tsp garlic powder

1 tsp onion powder

1 tsp paprika

¼ tsp chili powder

⅛ tsp cayenne pepper (optional)

1 tsp brown sugar

Salt and pepper, to taste

SPICY RANCH DIPPING SAUCE

¼ cup (60 ml) prepared ranch dressing

2 tbsp (30 ml) mayonnaise

1 tbsp (15 ml) sriracha, or to taste

FOR SERVING

2 tbsp (12 g) chopped green onion

Spicy Ranch Dipping Sauce

Carrot and celery sticks

Prepare the filling. Chop up your prepared mac 'n' cheese into smaller pieces so that it is easier to stuff. It's best to do so when the pasta is cold or at room temperature.

With a paper towel, pat the wings dry. Stuff the wings by loosening the skin around the drumette and flat areas (on the meatier side opposite of the bone) with your fingers/thumb to create a pocket that can be stuffed. Fill each wing with about ½ teaspoon of the mac 'n' cheese. Push the filling as far down as possible. Do not overstuff, and leave some room to close the flap.

In a small bowl, combine the garlic powder, onion powder, paprika, chili powder, cayenne (if using), brown sugar, salt and pepper. Sprinkle the prepared rub over the wings, coating evenly.

Preheat the grill or smoker to 350°F (180°C), indirect heat. Place the wings, stuffing side up, on the grill grates.

Grill the wings for 40 minutes or until they reach a minimum internal temperature of 165°F (75°C), or 190°F (90°C) if you like them well done. Flipping the wings is not recommended. Some filling will come out during the grilling process, which is not unusual.

Prepare the dipping sauce. In a small bowl, whisk together the ranch dressing, mayonnaise and sriracha.

Plate the wings and garnish them with green onion. Serve them with the Spicy Ranch Dipping Sauce and carrot and celery sticks.

*See image on page 151 (shown in the middle).

BUFFALO DIP STUFFED

Is it even game day without buffalo wings and buffalo chicken dip? This winning recipe combines your love of both for the perfect wings. It consists of a cheesy, creamy buffalo filling that is stuffed inside of a chicken wing. They are juicy, savory and full of flavor. To save time, feel free to use Frank's RedHot Buffalo Sauce as a substitute instead of making your own.

SERVINGS: 4

BUFFALO SAUCE
½ cup (120 ml) Frank's RedHot Original

2 tbsp (30 ml) honey

4 tbsp (56 g) unsalted butter

BUFFALO DIP
4 oz (120 g) cream cheese, softened

¼ cup (120 ml) Buffalo Sauce

⅓ cup (37 g) shredded cheddar cheese

¼ cup (60 ml) ranch dressing

2 lb (907 g) chicken wings, tips removed, drums and flats separated

1 tsp garlic powder

Salt and pepper, to taste

FOR SERVING
Blue cheese dressing

2 tbsp (12 g) chopped green onion

Carrot and celery sticks

Prepare the sauce. In a small saucepan, whisk together the hot sauce and honey over medium-low heat. Bring to a simmer and stir in the butter. Cook until the butter is melted and slightly reduced, about 2 minutes.

Make the Buffalo Dip by combining the cream cheese, Buffalo Sauce, cheddar cheese and ranch dressing.

With a paper towel, pat the wings dry. Stuff the wings by loosening the skin around the drumette and flat areas (on the meatier side opposite of the bone) with your fingers/thumb to create a pocket that can be stuffed. Fill each wing with about ½ teaspoon of the Buffalo Dip stuffing. Push the Buffalo Dip as far down as possible. Do not overstuff, and leave some room to close the flap.

In a small bowl, combine the garlic powder, salt and pepper. Sprinkle the prepared rub over the wings, coating evenly.

Preheat the grill or smoker to 350°F (180°C), indirect heat. Place wings, stuffing side up, on the grill grates.

Grill the wings for 40 minutes or until they reach a minimum internal temperature of 165°F (75°C), or 190°F (90°C) if you like them well done. Flipping the wings is not recommended. Some of the filling will come out during the grilling process, which is not unusual.

Brush the wings with the remaining Buffalo Sauce and place them back on grill grates for 5 to 10 minutes, until the sauce settles.

Plate the wings, drizzle with blue cheese dressing and garnish with green onion. Serve with carrot and celery sticks.

*See image on page 151 (shown on the bottom).

FLAMIN' HOT® CHEETOS®

Flamin' Hot Cheetos are one of my favorite crunchy and spicy snacks. Combine them with my love for crispy fried chicken and here we are. These wings have a crisp-tender texture with a cheesy and spicy finish, and after just one bite, you'll understand what the hype is all about. No egg or flour dredge is required. My Creamy Garlic Dill Dipping Sauce gives this recipe a perfect "cooling" finish.

SERVINGS: 4

1 (11-oz [310-g]) bag Flamin' Hot Cheetos

2 lb (907 g) chicken wings, tips removed, drums and flats separated

½ cup (120 ml) hot sauce, such as Frank's RedHot Original

2 tbsp (30 ml) ranch dressing

1 tbsp (15 ml) honey

CREAMY GARLIC DILL DIPPING SAUCE

¼ cup (60 ml) sour cream

2 tbsp (30 ml) mayonnaise

2 cloves garlic, minced

1 tbsp (3 g) chopped fresh dill

1 tsp grated Parmesan cheese

1 tsp freshly squeezed lemon juice

Salt and pepper, to taste

FOR SERVING

2 tbsp (12 g) chopped green onion

Creamy Garlic Dill Dipping Sauce

Place the Flamin' Hot Cheetos in a food processor and grind until they resemble breadcrumbs. Blend in batches, if needed. Alternatively, place the Cheetos in a large resealable plastic bag and crush with a rolling pin (see Note). Pour the Cheetos crumbs into a large bowl.

Place an oven-safe baking/cooling rack on top of a lined baking sheet. With a paper towel, pat the wings dry. In a medium bowl, combine the hot sauce, ranch dressing and honey. Dip each wing in the sauce, making sure that they are coated evenly. Shake off any excess. This will help the Cheetos stick to the wings. Place the wings in the Cheetos crumbs, pressing down and coating each side evenly. You want to keep the chip coating as dry as possible without too many clumps. Place the wings on the prepared baking rack, evenly spaced.

Preheat the grill or smoker to 350°F (180°C), indirect heat. Place the oven-safe rack with the wings directly on the grill grates.

Grill the wings for 40 minutes or until they reach a minimum internal temperature of 165°F (75°C), or 190°F (90°C) if you like them well done. There is no need to flip the wings.

Prepare the dipping sauce. In a small mixing bowl, combine all the ingredients. Cover and refrigerate before serving.

Plate the wings and garnish them with green onion. Serve them with the Creamy Garlic Dill Dipping Sauce.

NOTE: The trick to getting a perfectly crunchy coating with the Flamin' Hot Cheetos is to not over grind in a food processor. Doing so produces a dust that, although it tastes great, doesn't get very crispy. You want to leave some bigger pieces. The goal is to create a fried-like crunch.

RAMEN CRUSTED

Hands up if instant ramen was your go-to in college! It was and is quick, simple and flavorful, just like these ramen-crusted wings! The spice is right on these with a crispy crunch finish, no frying required. This combo might sound crazy, but once you take your first bite you'll be hooked. These wings are tender, juicy and mind-blowing!

SERVINGS: 4

2 (140-g [5-oz]) packages hot chicken flavor ramen or your favorite, crumbled

2 lb (907 g) chicken wings, tips removed, drums and flats separated

3 tbsp (45 ml) sambal oelek (chili paste)

2 tbsp (30 ml) hoisin sauce

SRIRACHA RANCH DIPPING SAUCE

2 tbsp (30 ml) sriracha

1 tbsp (15 ml) ranch dressing

FOR SERVING

Sesame seeds

2 tbsp (12 g) chopped green onion

Sriracha Ranch Dipping Sauce

Break apart the ramen noodles into a medium bowl with your hands. The pieces should be small enough that they stick to the wings and big enough that they keep their shape. Set aside the liquid sauce and flake packets included in the ramen. Prepare an oven-safe baking/cooling rack on top of a lined baking sheet. With a paper towel, pat the wings dry. Place the wings in a large mixing bowl and pour the sambal oelek and hoisin sauce over the top. Toss to coat evenly. This will help the ramen noodles stick to the wings. Coat each wing in ramen noodles by pressing down and coating each side evenly. Place the wings on the prepared baking/cooling rack, evenly spaced.

Preheat the grill or smoker to 350°F (180°C), indirect heat. Place the oven-safe baking/cooling rack with wings directly on grill grates.

Grill the wings for 40 minutes or until they reach a minimum internal temperature of 165°F (75°C), or 190°F (90°C) if you like them well done. There is no need to flip the wings.

Meanwhile, prepare the dipping sauce. In a small bowl, combine the sriracha and ranch dressing.

Pour the contents of the hot sauce packets into a small bowl. Plate the wings, brush with hot sauce and garnish them with the provided flakes, sesame seeds and green onion (see Note). Serve them with the Sriracha Ranch Dipping Sauce.

NOTE: Depending on your spice level tolerance, you can omit brushing the hot sauce on the wings. If you are using ramen that has a seasoning packet instead of a sauce packet, sprinkle the seasoning over the ramen after breaking it apart and toss to coat. You'll garnish them with the provided flakes and green onion.

EVERYTHING BUT THE BAGEL

Do you love everything bagels as much as I do? These wings will be a HUGE hit with anyone that tries them. They are coated in Dijon mustard to create a beautiful golden color and as something for the seasoning to stick to. They are paired with a delicious BBQ Mustard Dipping Sauce.

SERVINGS: 4

2 lb (907 g) chicken wings, tips removed, drums and flats separated

2 tbsp (16 g) dried minced garlic

1 tbsp (9 g) black sesame seeds

1 tbsp (9 g) white sesame seeds

1 tbsp (7 g) dried minced onion

½ tbsp (4 g) poppy seeds

½ tsp salt

¼ tsp black pepper

⅓ cup (80 ml) Dijon mustard

1 tbsp (15 ml) oil

2 tbsp (16 g) garlic powder

BBQ MUSTARD DIPPING SAUCE

¼ cup (60 ml) mayonnaise

1 tbsp (15 ml) yellow mustard

2 tsp (10 ml) Dijon mustard

2 tbsp (30 ml) your favorite BBQ sauce (I use Bull's-Eye™ original)

1–2 tbsp (15–30 ml) honey

2 tsp (10 ml) lemon juice

FOR SERVING

BBQ Mustard Dipping Sauce

Place an oven-safe baking/cooling rack on top of a lined baking sheet. With a paper towel, pat the wings dry. In a medium bowl, combine the dried minced garlic, black sesame seeds, white sesame seeds, dried minced onion, poppy seeds, salt and pepper. In another small bowl, combine the Dijon mustard, oil and garlic powder; add the liquid mixture to the bowl with the wings. Toss until they are completely coated.

Toss or roll the wings in 4 to 5 tablespoons (32 to 40 g) of the seasoning mixture. Place the wings on the prepared baking/cooling rack, evenly spaced. Sprinkle any additional seasoning over the wings, if desired.

Preheat the grill or smoker to 350°F (180°C), indirect heat. Place the oven-safe baking/cooling rack with wings directly on the grill grates.

Grill the wings for 40 minutes or until they reach a minimum internal temperature of 165°F (75°C), or 190°F (90°C) if you like them well done, flipping them halfway through the cooking time.

Meanwhile, prepare the dipping sauce. In a small bowl, combine the mayonnaise, yellow mustard, Dijon mustard, BBQ sauce, honey and lemon juice.

Plate the wings and serve them with the BBQ Mustard Dipping Sauce.

FRENCH TOAST

These chicken wings are a game changer! Yes, they taste just like French toast. There's something special about making rich and delicious French toast on a lazy weekend morning. These wings are sweet, savory and drizzled with maple syrup for a perfect finish. Treat your guests to these crave-worthy wings at your next get-together.

SERVINGS: 4

2 lb (907 g) chicken wings, tips removed, drums and flats separated

2 tbsp (28 g) brown sugar

1½ tsp (5 g) ground cinnamon

Salt, to taste

SPICY MAPLE-MUSTARD DIPPING SAUCE

½ cup (120 ml) mayonnaise

¼ cup (60 ml) yellow mustard

1 tsp sriracha

¼ cup (60 ml) maple syrup

½ tsp garlic powder

Salt and pepper, to taste

FOR SERVING

Drizzle of maple syrup

2 tbsp (12 g) chopped green onion (optional)

Spicy Maple-Mustard Dipping Sauce

Carrot and celery sticks

With a paper towel, pat the wings dry. In a small bowl, combine the brown sugar, ground cinnamon and salt. Sprinkle the prepared rub over the wings, coating evenly.

Preheat the grill or smoker to 350°F (180°C), indirect heat.

Grill the wings for 40 minutes or until they reach a minimum internal temperature of 165°F (75°C), or 190°F (90°C) if you like them well done, flipping them halfway through the cooking time. To crisp the skin, move the wings to the direct heat side of the grill, turning occasionally, until the skin is dark golden or to your liking.

Meanwhile, prepare the sauce. In a small bowl, whisk to combine the mayonnaise, yellow mustard, sriracha, maple syrup, garlic powder, salt and pepper.

Plate the wings and drizzle them with maple syrup and garnish them with green onion, if desired. Serve them with the Spicy Maple-Mustard Dipping Sauce and carrot and celery sticks.

CHICKEN AND WAFFLE

2 lb (907 g) chicken wings, tips removed, drums and flats separated

1 tsp paprika

2 tsp (10 g) brown sugar

1 tsp garlic powder

1 tsp onion powder

1/8 tsp cayenne pepper

1/4 tsp chili powder

Salt and pepper, to taste

1 cup (120 g) Bisquick® original baking mix

1/2 cup (120 ml) milk

1 egg

WAFFLE SAUCE

1/4 cup (56 g) unsalted butter, melted

1/4 cup (60 ml) Frank's RedHot Original

1/4 cup (60 ml) maple syrup

FOR SERVING

4 strips thinly cut bacon, diced and fried

Waffle Sauce

Brunch game is strong with these chicken wings! They are sweet, savory, crunchy and topped with bacon. Yes, it's possible to put wings inside a waffle. This is one of my favorite twists on a classic, and it is perfectly finished with crispy bacon and a spicy maple syrup drizzle. Impress your friends and family with this INSANELY delicious recipe.

SERVINGS: 4

With a paper towel, pat the wings dry. In a small bowl, combine the paprika, brown sugar, garlic powder, onion powder, cayenne, chili powder, salt and pepper. Sprinkle the prepared rub over the wings, coating evenly.

Preheat the grill or smoker to 350°F (180°C), indirect heat.

Grill the wings for 40 minutes or until they reach a minimum internal temperature of 165°F (75°C), or 190°F (90°C) if you like them well done, flipping them halfway through the cooking time. To crisp the skin, move the wings to the direct heat side of the grill, turning occasionally, until the skin is dark golden or to your liking.

Meanwhile, prepare the sauce. In a large bowl, stir together the warm melted butter, hot sauce and maple syrup.

Prepare the batter. In a medium bowl, whisk to combine the Bisquick, milk and egg.

Transfer the wings to a bowl and toss with the Waffle Sauce until completely coated. Place the wings back on the grill grates for about 5 minutes, or until the sauce settles.

Preheat a waffle iron to high and spray with nonstick spray. Start with all the drumettes, then the flats, cooking them separately. Dip each wing in the batter, letting any excess drip off. The lighter the coating, the better. Place the wings on the corners of the waffle iron with the ends hanging out. Press down and cook until the tops of the waffles are golden brown, 3 to 4 minutes. Work in batches.

Plate the wings and garnish them with bacon, then drizzle with some of the Waffle Sauce. Serve with leftover sauce.

*See image on page 161 (shown on the bottom right).

OREO AND BACON

Oreo cookie and bacon chicken wings! Do I have your attention? These are simple to make and your next obsession. Get the party and conversation started with this recipe. The cookie crumble makes these wings crispy, and the bacon crumbs come in for a savory finish.

SERVINGS: 4

2 lb (907 g) chicken wings, tips removed, drums and flats separated

Your favorite BBQ rub (I use Pit Boss® Ale House Beer Can Chicken)

1½ cups (159 g) crushed Golden Oreos®

½ cup (128 g) smooth peanut butter

4–6 slices thin-cut bacon, chopped into small pieces

FOR SERVING

Bacon crumbs

Ranch or blue cheese dressing

Carrot and celery sticks

Place an oven-safe baking/cooling rack on top of a lined baking sheet. With a paper towel, pat the wings dry. Sprinkle your favorite rub over the wings, coating evenly. Set aside. Place the crushed Oreos in a large bowl. Place the wings in a separate large bowl and top with the peanut butter. Toss to coat; this will help the cookie crumbs stick to the wings. Place the wings in the Golden Oreo crumbs, pressing down and coating each side evenly. Then, place the wings on the prepared baking/cooling rack, evenly spaced.

Preheat the grill or smoker to 350°F (180°C), indirect heat. Place the oven-safe baking/cooling rack with the wings directly on the grill grates.

Grill the wings for 40 minutes or until they reach a minimum internal temperature of 165°F (75°C), or 190°F (90°C) if you like them well done. There is no need to flip the wings.

Meanwhile, fry the bacon. In a medium saucepan over medium heat, fry the bacon for 5 to 7 minutes, or until crispy. Strain the grease.

Plate the wings and garnish them with bacon crumbs. Serve them with ranch or blue cheese dressing for dipping and carrot and celery sticks.

*See image on page 161 (shown on the bottom left).

PEANUT BUTTER AND JELLY

Peanut butter and jelly sandwiches are a childhood classic. Let's step it up a notch and add bacon. Yes, that's right, bacon! Trust me, this will blow your mind. Combine that with your love of chicken wings and you have the perfect pairing of sweet and spice. These peanut butter and jelly wings will be a hit at your table! If you love peanut satay, these are a MUST try.

SERVINGS: 4

2 lb (907 g) chicken wings, tips removed, drums and flats separated

2 tbsp (25 g) your favorite BBQ seasoning (I use Louisiana Grills Sweet Heat)

3 strips fried bacon, crumbled (bacon grease reserved)

PEANUT BUTTER AND JELLY SAUCE

⅛ cup (32 g) smooth peanut butter

¼ cup (60 ml) strawberry jelly or any jelly

1 tsp sriracha

1 tsp low sodium soy sauce

4 tsp (20 ml) reserved bacon grease

FOR SERVING

Bacon crumbs

2 tbsp (18 g) chopped peanuts

2 tbsp (12 g) chopped green onion

Leftover Peanut Butter and Jelly Sauce

Ranch dressing (optional)

With a paper towel, pat the wings dry. Season the wings with your favorite BBQ seasoning, coating evenly.

Preheat the grill or smoker to 350°F (180°C), indirect heat.

Grill the wings for 40 minutes or until they reach a minimum internal temperature of 165°F (75°C), or 190°F (90°C) if you like them well done, flipping them halfway through the cooking time. To crisp the skin, move the wings to the direct heat side of the grill, turning occasionally, until the skin is dark golden or to your liking.

Meanwhile, prepare the sauce. In a small pot, combine the peanut butter, jelly, sriracha, soy sauce and bacon grease. Cook over low heat and stir until the sauce is a smooth, even consistency. Keep warm until needed.

Transfer the wings to a bowl and toss with the Peanut Butter and Jelly Sauce until completely coated. Plate the wings and garnish them with bacon crumbs, chopped peanuts and green onion. Serve them with leftover sauce or ranch dressing.

STRAWBERRY CHEESECAKE

What is your favorite dessert? Mine is strawberry cheesecake; it brings me back to my childhood. My mom always made it for special occasions or when it was requested, and these chicken wings have all those familiar flavors. The first time I made these, they quickly disappeared. They are sweet, saucy and topped with graham cracker crumbles. These will blow your mind—trust me.

SERVINGS: 4

2 lb (907 g) chicken wings, tips removed, drums and flats separated

1 tsp paprika

1 tsp garlic powder

1 tsp onion powder

¼ tsp chili powder

1 tsp brown sugar

Salt and pepper, to taste

STRAWBERRY BBQ SAUCE

⅓ cup (80 ml) your favorite BBQ sauce (I use Bull's-Eye Original)

¼ cup (60 ml) strawberry jam

⅛ tsp ground cinnamon

½ tsp garlic powder

Salt, to taste

CHEESECAKE DIPPING SAUCE

¼ cup (58 g) mascarpone cheese or cream cheese, at room temperature

¼ cup (60 ml) sour cream

½ tsp pure vanilla extract

1–2 tsp (3–6 g) icing sugar

FOR SERVING

Graham cracker crumbs

Halved fresh strawberries

Cheesecake Dipping Sauce

With a paper towel, pat the wings dry. In a small bowl, combine the paprika, garlic powder, onion powder, chili powder, brown sugar, salt and pepper. Sprinkle the prepared rub over the wings, coating evenly.

Preheat the grill or smoker to 350°F (180°C), indirect heat.

Grill the wings for 40 minutes or until they reach a minimum internal temperature of 165°F (75°C), or 190°F (90°C) if you like them well done, flipping them halfway through the cooking time. To crisp the skin, move the wings to the direct heat side of the grill, turning occasionally, until the skin is dark golden or to your liking.

Meanwhile, prepare the sauce. In a small saucepan over medium heat, combine the BBQ sauce, strawberry jam, ground cinnamon, garlic powder and salt. Stir frequently and bring to a boil. Reduce the heat to low and simmer for about 5 minutes.

Prepare the dipping sauce. In a small bowl, whisk to combine the mascarpone cheese, sour cream, vanilla extract and icing sugar.

Transfer the wings to a bowl and toss with the Strawberry BBQ Sauce until completely coated. Plate the wings and garnish them with graham cracker crumbs and strawberries and serve them with the Cheesecake Dipping Sauce.

BIG MAC®–STYLE STUFFED

If chicken wings were a burger, they would be a Big Mac–style stuffed creation. One of my favorite fast-food burgers is the Big Mac, so naturally I had to re-create it in the form of wings. I guess you can say McChicken® meets Big Mac? Take a big bite to get all that flavor in, you'll be hooked. All that flavor stuffed into a wing? Yes, it's possible.

SERVINGS: 4

2 lb (907 g) chicken wings, tips removed, drums and flats separated

2 cups (480 ml) dill pickle juice or enough to cover wings

½ tsp dry dill

1 tsp garlic powder

1 tsp onion powder

1 tsp paprika

1 tsp chili powder

1 tsp brown sugar

Salt and pepper, to taste

BIG MAC–STYLE FILLING

1 tbsp (15 ml) vegetable oil

1 tbsp (10 g) finely chopped white onion

1 cup (217 g) ground beef

Salt and pepper, to taste

¼ cup (36 g) diced pickles

1 cup (112 g) shredded cheddar cheese

COMEBACK DIPPING SAUCE

¾ cup (180 ml) mayonnaise

2 tsp (10 ml) yellow mustard

2 tbsp (30 g) sweet pickle relish

1 tbsp (15 ml) white vinegar

½ tsp garlic powder

½ tsp onion powder

½–1 tsp paprika

FOR SERVING

Sesame seeds

Hamburger pickle slices

Comeback Dipping Sauce

With a paper towel, pat the wings dry. Place the wings in a shallow dish or resealable plastic bag and pour enough pickle juice to cover the wings. Cover and refrigerate for 3 to 6 hours or overnight, if time permits (the longer the better for best flavor results).

Meanwhile, prepare the filling. In a medium pan over medium-high heat, heat the oil and add the onion. Sauté until fragrant and translucent, 2 to 3 minutes. Add the ground beef and season with salt and pepper. Cook until no longer pink, breaking apart and stirring as the meat cooks, about 10 minutes. Set aside and let cool.

Combine the diced pickles and shredded cheddar cheese with the cooled ground beef.

Stuff the wings by loosening the skin around the drumette and flat areas (on the meatier side opposite of the bone) with your fingers/thumb to create a pocket that can be stuffed. Fill each wing with about ½ teaspoon of the Big Mac–Style Filling. Push the filling as far down as possible. Do not overstuff, and leave some room to close the flap.

In a small bowl, combine the dry dill, garlic powder, onion powder, paprika, chili powder, brown sugar, salt and pepper. Remove the wings from the marinade and pat them dry with a paper towel. Discard the marinade. Sprinkle the prepared rub over the wings, coating evenly.

Preheat the grill or smoker to 350°F (180°C), indirect heat. Place the wings, stuffing side up, on the grill grates.

Grill the wings for 40 minutes or until they reach a minimum internal temperature of 165°F (75°C), or 190°F (90°C) if you like them well done. Flipping the wings is not recommended. Some filling will come out during the grilling process, which is not unusual.

Prepare the dipping sauce. In a small bowl, whisk together the mayonnaise, yellow mustard, pickle relish, white vinegar, garlic powder, onion powder and paprika.

Plate the wings and garnish them with sesame seeds. Serve them with hamburger pickle slices and Comeback Dipping Sauce.

*See image on page 148.

BUTTER POPCORN

These Butter Popcorn—crusted chicken wings will be your new favorite movie night snack. They are tender, juicy, have a crunchy texture and are drizzled with a rich, buttery mixture for a finger-licking finish! These wings take "popcorn chicken" to a whole new level. Movie night will never be the same.

SERVINGS: 4

NOTE: Do not over grind the popcorn in a food processor. Doing so gives a dust that, although it tastes great, doesn't get very crispy. You'll want to leave some bigger pieces for crunchy results.

2 lb (907 g) chicken wings, tips removed, drums and flats separated

1 tsp smoked paprika

1 tsp garlic powder

1 tsp onion powder

1 tsp chili powder

1 tsp brown sugar

Salt and pepper, to taste (if your popcorn is salty, use less salt)

4–6 cups (32–48 g) butter popcorn, popped (I use Orville Redenbacher®)

2 tsp (6 g) garlic powder

2 cups (250 g) all-purpose flour

3 eggs, beaten

¼ cup (56 g) unsalted butter

1 tbsp (8 g) grated Parmesan cheese

FOR SERVING

Ranch or Caesar dressing

Carrot and celery sticks

Place an oven-safe baking/cooling rack on top of a lined baking sheet. With a paper towel, pat the wings dry. In a small bowl, combine the smoked paprika, garlic powder, onion powder, chili powder, brown sugar, salt and pepper. Sprinkle the prepared rub over the wings, coating evenly. Set aside.

Place the popped popcorn and garlic powder in a food processor and pulse until they resemble breadcrumbs—not dust (see Note). Blend in batches. Pour the popcorn crumbs into a large bowl. Place the flour in a separate shallow bowl and whisk the eggs in another bowl. Coat each wing in flour (shake off the excess), dip in the egg mixture and then coat in the popcorn mixture, pressing down and coating each side evenly. You want to keep the popcorn coating as dry as possible without too many clumps. Place the wings on the prepared baking/cooling rack, evenly spaced.

Preheat the grill or smoker to 350°F (180°C), indirect heat. Place the oven-safe baking/cooling rack with the wings directly on the grill grates.

Grill the wings for 40 minutes or until they reach a minimum internal temperature of 165°F (75°C), or 190°F (90°C) if you like them well done. There is no need to flip the wings.

Meanwhile, melt the butter. In a small bowl, stir together the warm melted butter and Parmesan cheese. Plate the wings and drizzle them with the Parmesan-butter mixture. Serve them with ranch or Caesar dressing for dipping and carrot and celery sticks.

PRETZEL CRUSTED

What comes to mind when you think of pretzels? For me, it's mustard and beer, which are the key ingredients to these wings. These chicken wings are crunchy (which is the best part), tender, juicy and mind-blowing! Trust me when I tell you these will be a hit!

SERVINGS: 4

2 lb (907 g) chicken wings, tips removed, drums and flats separated

Your favorite beer

1 tsp paprika

2 tsp brown sugar

1 tsp garlic powder

1 tsp onion powder

¼ tsp chili powder

Black pepper, to taste

2 cups (180 g) crushed pretzel sticks (I use Rold Gold® pretzel sticks)

²/₃ cup (160 ml) yellow mustard

HONEY MUSTARD DIPPING SAUCE

¼ cup (60 ml) mayonnaise

1 tbsp (15 ml) yellow mustard

2 tsp (10 ml) Dijon mustard

2 tbsp (30 ml) BBQ sauce, such as Bull's-Eye original or your favorite

1–2 tbsp (15–30 ml) honey

2 tsp (10 ml) lemon juice

FOR SERVING

Honey Mustard Dipping Sauce

With a paper towel, pat the wings dry. Place the wings in a shallow dish or resealable plastic bag and pour in enough beer to cover. Cover and refrigerate for a minimum of 2 hours or overnight (the longer the better for best flavor results).

Place an oven-safe baking/cooling rack on top of a lined baking sheet. In a small bowl, combine the paprika, brown sugar, garlic powder, onion powder, chili powder and black pepper. Place the crushed pretzels in a large bowl. Season the crushed pretzels with the combined rub. Place the mustard in a separate medium bowl. Dip each wing in mustard, making sure that they are coated evenly. Shake off any excess sauce. This will help the pretzels stick to the wings. Next, place the wings in the crushed pretzels, pressing down and coating each side evenly. Then, place the wings on the prepared baking/cooling rack, evenly spaced.

Preheat the grill or smoker to 350°F (180°C), indirect heat. Place the oven-safe baking/cooling rack with the wings directly on the grill grates.

Grill the wings for 40 minutes or until they reach a minimum internal temperature of 165°F (75°C), or 190°F (90°C) if you like them well done. There is no need to flip the wings.

Meanwhile, prepare the dipping sauce. In a small bowl, combine the mayonnaise, yellow mustard, Dijon mustard, BBQ sauce, honey and lemon juice.

Plate the wings and drizzle some Honey Mustard Dipping Sauce over the wings or simply serve for dipping.

*See image on page 170 (shown in the middle).

CHEEZ-IT® CRUSTED

Do you like fried chicken? These chicken wings have the same juicy, tender and perfectly crispy bite right off the grill. They are simple to make with only a few ingredients and are out-of-this-world delicious! This is one of my go-to recipes paired with a delicious Ranch-Dill Dipping Sauce.

SERVINGS: 4

2 cups (120 g) Cheez-It original crackers

1 tsp garlic powder

1 tsp onion powder

2 tbsp (15 g) grated Parmesan cheese

½ cup (120 ml) Frank's RedHot Original

¼ cup (60 ml) ranch dressing

2 lb (907 g) chicken wings, tips removed, drums and flats separated

RANCH-DILL DIPPING SAUCE

¼ cup (60 ml) mayonnaise

¼ cup (60 ml) sour cream

1 tbsp (14 g) ranch seasoning mix (I use Hidden Valley)

1 tsp fresh minced dill

¼ tsp onion powder

⅛ tsp garlic powder

FOR SERVING

2 tbsp (12 g) chopped green onion

Ranch-Dill Dipping Sauce

Carrot and celery sticks

In a food processor or in a large resealable bag with a rolling pin, crush the Cheez-It crackers, until coarsely ground. Place them in a large bowl and combine with the garlic powder, onion powder and Parmesan cheese. In a separate medium bowl, combine the hot sauce and ranch dressing.

Place an oven-safe baking/cooling rack on top of a lined baking sheet. With a paper towel, pat the wings dry. Dip each wing in the hot sauce–ranch mixture, making sure that they are coated evenly. Shake off any excess sauce. This will help the cracker mix stick to the wings. Next, place the wings in the crushed Cheez-It cracker mix, pressing down and coating each side evenly. Then, place the wings on the prepared baking/cooling rack, evenly spaced.

Preheat the grill or smoker to 350°F (180°C), indirect heat. Place the oven-safe baking/cooling rack with the wings directly on the grill grates.

Grill the wings for 40 minutes or until they reach a minimum internal temperature of 165°F (75°C), or 190°F (90°C) if you like them well done. There is no need to flip the wings.

Meanwhile, prepare the dipping sauce. In a small bowl, combine the mayonnaise, sour cream, ranch seasoning mix, fresh dill, onion powder and garlic powder.

Plate the wings and garnish them with green onion. Serve them with Ranch-Dill Dipping Sauce and carrot and celery sticks.

*See image on page 170 (shown on the bottom).

LET'S GET TIPSY

It's 5 o'clock somewhere and you need a chicken wing in one hand and a cocktail in the other. It's been a long week, so let's unwind with some classic cocktail–inspired chicken wings. They are sweet, sticky, boozy and packed with flavor. Don't leave any of these recipes out of happy hour.

CHOCOLATE STOUT

Disclaimer: No chocolate was used in the making of these chicken wings. The wildly delicious combo of Guinness® beer, brown sugar and balsamic vinegar create a chocolate flavor with a hint of spice from the hot sauce. These are going to be an instant hit at any gathering, so be sure to keep some aside for yourself.

SERVINGS: 4

2 lb (907 g) chicken wings, tips removed, drums and flats separated

1 tsp garlic powder

1 tsp onion powder

1 tsp paprika

¼ tsp chili powder

2 tsp (8 g) brown sugar

⅛ tsp cayenne pepper

Salt and pepper, to taste

CHOCOLATE STOUT SAUCE

1 tbsp (15 ml) vegetable oil

¼ cup (40 g) diced white onion

1 clove garlic, minced

¼ tsp Tabasco hot sauce (optional)

¼ cup (60 ml) balsamic vinegar

¼ cup (60 ml) water

⅓ cup (73 g) brown sugar

1 tbsp (16 g) tomato paste

1 tsp Worcestershire sauce, or to taste

½ cup (120 ml) Guinness beer stout, or another stout that has chocolate/vanilla notes

Salt and pepper, to taste

FOR SERVING

2 tbsp (12 g) chopped green onion

Leftover Chocolate Stout Sauce

Ranch dressing (optional)

Carrot and celery sticks

With a paper towel, pat the wings dry. In a small bowl, combine the garlic powder, onion powder, paprika, chili powder, brown sugar, cayenne pepper, salt and pepper. Sprinkle the prepared rub over the wings, coating evenly.

Preheat the grill or smoker to 350°F (180°C), indirect heat.

Grill the wings for 40 minutes or until they reach a minimum internal temperature of 165°F (75°C), or 190°F (90°C) if you like them well done, flipping them halfway through the cooking time. To crisp the skin, move the wings to the direct heat side of the grill, turning occasionally, until the skin is dark golden or to your liking.

Meanwhile, prepare the sauce. In a small saucepan, heat the oil over medium heat. Add the onion and minced garlic. Stir frequently and sauté until the onion and garlic start to brown, 2 to 3 minutes. Next, add the Tabasco (if using), balsamic vinegar, water, brown sugar, tomato paste, Worcestershire sauce and Guinness. Bring to a boil, then reduce heat to a simmer. Simmer for about 5 minutes or until the sauce is thickened. Strain the sauce over a bowl, then season to taste with salt and pepper.

Transfer the wings to a bowl and toss them with the Chocolate Stout Sauce until completely coated. Place the wings back on the grill grates for about 5 minutes, until the sauce settles, or serve immediately. Plate the wings and garnish them with green onion. Serve them with leftover sauce and/or ranch dressing and carrot and celery sticks.

FIREBALL® WHISKEY

These Fireball Whiskey chicken wings will be the talk of the town, and you'll wish you made more. They are sweet, tangy and as spicy as you want them to be. The Fireball BBQ sauce is perfect to make ahead of time and heat up when ready to serve.

SERVINGS: 4

2 lb (907 g) chicken wings, tips removed, drums and flats separated

FIREBALL MARINADE
1 tbsp (15 ml) Fireball Whiskey

2–3 tbsp (30–45 ml) pineapple juice

1 tbsp (14 g) brown sugar

2 tsp (6 g) chili powder

1 tsp garlic powder

1 tsp paprika

1 tsp ground cinnamon

¼ tsp cayenne pepper (optional)

Salt and pepper, to taste

FIREBALL WHISKEY SAUCE
½ cup (120 ml) Fireball Whiskey

¼ cup (60 ml) pineapple juice

½ cup (120 ml) ketchup

2 tbsp (30 ml) apple cider vinegar

2 tbsp (30 ml) Worcestershire sauce

2 cloves garlic, minced

2 tbsp (28 g) brown sugar

Salt and pepper, to taste

FOR SERVING
2 tbsp (12 g) chopped green onion

Leftover Fireball Whiskey Sauce

Ranch dressing (optional)

With a paper towel, pat the wings dry. Place the wings in a shallow dish or resealable plastic bag. In a medium bowl, whisk together the Fireball whiskey, pineapple juice, brown sugar, chili powder, garlic powder, paprika, cinnamon, cayenne (if using), salt and pepper. Pour the marinade over the wings and toss to coat. Cover and refrigerate for 1 to 8 hours (the longer the better).

Preheat the grill or smoker to 350°F (180°C), indirect heat.

Grill the wings for 40 minutes or until they reach a minimum internal temperature of 165°F (75°C), or 190°F (90°C) if you like them well done, flipping them halfway through the cooking time. To crisp the skin, move the wings to the direct heat side of the grill, turning occasionally, until the skin is dark golden or to your liking.

Meanwhile, prepare the sauce. In a medium saucepan over medium heat, whisk the Fireball whiskey, pineapple juice, ketchup, apple cider vinegar, Worcestershire sauce, garlic, brown sugar, salt and pepper. Bring to a boil, stirring frequently. Reduce the heat to low and simmer for 10 to 15 minutes or until the sauce has thickened.

Transfer the wings to a bowl and toss with the Fireball Whiskey Sauce to coat. Place the wings back on the grill grates for 5 to 10 minutes, until the sauce settles, or serve immediately. Plate the wings and garnish them with green onion. Serve them with leftover sauce and/or ranch dressing.

BBQ BOURBON

Does it get any better than BBQ, bourbon and chicken wings grilled to perfection? My BBQ Bourbon Sauce makes these wings irresistibly delicious and a must-have at any backyard BBQ. It's sweet, sticky, boozy and packed with flavor.

SERVINGS: 4

2 lb (907 g) chicken wings, tips removed, drums and flats separated

Your favorite BBQ rub (I use Pit Boss Ale House Beer Can Chicken rub)

BBQ BOURBON SAUCE

1½ cups (360 ml) ketchup

¾ cup (180 ml) bourbon whiskey (I use Maker's Mark)

2 tbsp (32 g) tomato paste

¼ cup (60 ml) apple cider vinegar

2 tbsp (30 ml) Worcestershire sauce

1 tbsp (15 ml) low-sodium soy sauce

1 tsp yellow mustard

1 tbsp (15 ml) honey

1 tsp smoked paprika

1 tsp garlic powder

1 tsp onion powder

1 tsp chili powder

Splash of hot sauce (I use Tabasco; optional)

Salt and pepper, to taste

FOR SERVING

Ranch or blue cheese dressing

Carrot and celery sticks

With a paper towel, pat the wings dry. Sprinkle your favorite rub over the wings, coating evenly.

Preheat the grill or smoker to 350°F (180°C), indirect heat.

Grill the wings for 40 minutes or until they reach a minimum internal temperature of 165°F (75°C), or 190°F (90°C) if you like them well done, flipping them halfway through the cooking time. To crisp the skin, move the wings to the direct heat side of the grill, turning occasionally, until the skin is dark golden or to your liking.

Meanwhile, prepare the sauce. In a large saucepan over medium heat, whisk together the ketchup, bourbon, tomato paste, apple cider vinegar, Worcestershire sauce, soy sauce, mustard, honey, smoked paprika, garlic powder, onion powder, chili powder, hot sauce (if using), salt and pepper. Bring to a boil, stirring occasionally. Reduce heat to medium-low and simmer for 15 to 20 minutes, stirring frequently.

Transfer the wings to a bowl and toss with the BBQ Bourbon Sauce until completely coated. Place the wings back on the grill grates for 5 to 10 minutes, until the sauce settles, or serve immediately. Serve them with ranch or blue cheese dressing for dipping and carrot and celery sticks.

*See image on page 178 (shown on the top).

OLD FASHIONED

An Old Fashioned is a timeless cocktail that is popular among whiskey lovers. Let's get happy hour started with one and some delicious wings! These wings have all those familiar flavors that will have you craving more once they're gone. Don't leave these out of cocktail hour.

SERVINGS: 4

2 lb (907 g) chicken wings, tips removed, drums and flats separated

1 tsp paprika

2 tsp (10 g) brown sugar

1 tsp garlic powder

1 tsp onion powder

¼ tsp chili powder

⅛ tsp cayenne pepper

Salt and pepper, to taste

OLD FASHIONED SAUCE

½ cup (120 ml) orange juice

1 tsp cornstarch

2 oz (60 ml) bourbon

1 tsp maple syrup

¼ cup (60 ml) cherry juice

2 tbsp (24 g) brown sugar

Dash of bitters

Salt and pepper, to taste

FOR SERVING

Orange zest

Leftover Old Fashioned Sauce

Ranch dressing (optional)

Carrot and celery sticks

With a paper towel, pat the wings dry. In a small bowl, combine the paprika, brown sugar, garlic powder, onion powder, chili powder, cayenne, salt and pepper. Sprinkle the prepared rub over the wings, coating evenly.

Preheat the grill or smoker to 350°F (180°C), indirect heat.

Grill the wings for 40 minutes or until they reach a minimum internal temperature of 165°F (75°C), or 190°F (90°C) if you like them well done, flipping them halfway through the cooking time. To crisp the skin, move the wings to the direct heat side of the grill, turning occasionally, until the skin is dark golden or to your liking.

Meanwhile, prepare the sauce. In a small bowl, whisk together the orange juice and cornstarch to form a smooth slurry. In a medium saucepan over medium heat, whisk together the bourbon, maple syrup, cherry juice, brown sugar, bitters, salt, pepper and the slurry. Bring to a boil, stirring occasionally. Reduce heat to low and simmer for about 10 minutes or until the sauce reduces and thickens, stirring frequently.

Transfer the wings to a bowl and toss with the Old Fashioned Sauce until completely coated. Place the wings back on the grill grates for 5 to 10 minutes, until the sauce settles, or serve immediately. Garnish them with orange zest and serve them with the leftover sauce and/or ranch dressing for dipping and carrot and celery sticks.

*See image on page 178 (shown on the bottom left).

BLOODY MARY

These Bloody Mary chicken wings embrace the classic brunch cocktail of vodka, tomato juice, Worcestershire sauce and hot sauce. They are marinated and later tossed in a mouth-watering Bloody Mary Sauce that packs a punch. Reduce the hot sauce if you prefer a milder marinade and sauce. Pair these delectable wings with a Bloody Mary cocktail.

SERVINGS: 4

2 lb (907 g) chicken wings, tips removed, drums and flats separated

½ tbsp (7 ml) extra-virgin olive oil

Celery salt, to taste

Pepper, to taste

1 tsp garlic powder

1 tsp onion powder

BLOODY MARY MARINADE AND SAUCE

2 cups (480 ml) tomato juice

⅓ cup (80 ml) vodka

2 tbsp (30 ml) pickle juice

Juice of ½ lemon

½ tbsp (8 g) prepared horseradish

1 tbsp (15 ml) Tabasco, or less depending on your spice level preference

½ tbsp (7 ml) Worcestershire sauce

¼ cup (55 g) brown sugar

Salt and pepper, to taste

FOR SERVING

2 tbsp (12 g) chopped green onion

Blue cheese dressing

Celery sticks

With a paper towel, pat the wings dry. Place the wings in a large bowl and drizzle in the olive oil. Season with the celery salt, pepper, garlic powder and onion powder. Toss to coat and set aside for about 20 minutes. Prepare the marinade. In another large bowl, combine the tomato juice, vodka, pickle juice, lemon juice, horseradish, Tabasco, Worcestershire sauce, brown sugar, salt and pepper. Pour the mixture over the wings until fully submerged. Keep the rest aside to make the sauce. Cover the wings and refrigerate for 1 to 2 hours. Shake off any excess and discard the marinade.

Preheat the grill or smoker to 350°F (180°C), indirect heat.

Grill the wings for 40 minutes or until they reach a minimum internal temperature of 165°F (75°C), or 190°F (90°C) if you like them well done, flipping them halfway through the cooking time. To crisp the skin, move the wings to the direct heat side of the grill, turning occasionally, until the skin is dark golden or to your liking.

Meanwhile, prepare the sauce. In a small saucepan over medium heat, add the Bloody Mary mixture. Bring to a boil and reduce the heat to low. Simmer until the sauce has reduced by half, 10 to 15 minutes.

Transfer the wings to a bowl and toss with the Bloody Mary Sauce until completely coated. Place them back on the grill grates for 5 to 10 minutes, or until the sauce settles. Plate the wings and serve them with blue cheese dressing for dipping and celery sticks.

TACOS AND TEQUILA

These Taco and Tequila chicken wings are seasoned with my taco rub and tossed in an irresistibly delicious sticky, sweet and citrus-flavored Tacos and Tequila Sauce. Can this combo get any better? These are sure to be a crowd-pleaser and perfect as an appetizer or a quick snack. They make the perfect companion to a margarita.

SERVINGS: 4

2 lb (907 g) chicken wings, tips removed, drums and flats separated

2 tsp (6 g) chili powder

½ tsp ground cumin

½ tsp garlic powder

½ tsp onion powder

½ tsp paprika

¼ tsp oregano

¼ tsp cayenne pepper

1 tsp cornstarch

Salt and pepper, to taste

TACOS AND TEQUILA SAUCE

¾ cup (180 ml) tequila

½ cup (120 ml) honey

2 tbsp (30 ml) hot sauce, or to taste (I use Frank's RedHot Original)

2 tbsp (30 ml) freshly squeezed lime juice

2 tbsp (30 ml) freshly squeezed orange juice

1 tbsp (7 g) prepared seasoning

FOR SERVING

2 tbsp (2 g) chopped cilantro

Lime wedges

Leftover Tacos and Tequila Sauce

Ranch dressing (optional)

With a paper towel, pat the wings dry. In a small bowl, combine the chili powder, cumin, garlic powder, onion powder, paprika, oregano, cayenne, cornstarch, salt and pepper. Reserve 1 tablespoon (11 g) of the seasoning for the sauce. Sprinkle the remaining prepared rub over the wings, coating evenly.

Preheat the grill or smoker to 350°F (180°C), indirect heat.

Grill the wings for 40 minutes or until they reach a minimum internal temperature of 165°F (75°C), or 190°F (90°C) if you like them well done, flipping them halfway through the cooking time. To crisp the skin, move the wings to the direct heat side of the grill, turning occasionally, until the skin is dark golden or to your liking.

Meanwhile, prepare the sauce. In a small saucepan over medium heat, whisk together the tequila, honey, hot sauce, lime juice, orange juice and prepared seasoning. Bring to a boil and turn down the heat to low. Simmer for about 20 minutes until the sauce has thickened, stirring occasionally.

Transfer the wings to a bowl and toss with the Tacos and Tequila Sauce until completely coated. Place the wings back on the grill grates for 5 to 10 minutes, until the sauce settles, or serve immediately. Plate and garnish them with cilantro. Serve them with lime wedges, leftover sauce and/ or ranch dressing for dipping.

MINGLING MOJITO

If you're inviting me to a cocktail party, I'm bringing these Mingling Mojito chicken wings. Why not turn this trendy classic cocktail into a wing sauce? They are sweet and citrusy with hints of rum and mint. Your guests will be impressed and asking for more. Serve them with a side of Mojito.

SERVINGS: 4

2 lb (907 g) chicken wings, tips removed, drums and flats separated

MOJITO MARINADE
½ cup (120 ml) white rum (I use Bacardi®)

Juice of 1 lime

1 tbsp (15 ml) freshly squeezed orange juice

1 clove garlic, minced

1 tsp onion powder

1 tbsp (14 g) brown sugar

½ tsp crushed red pepper flakes

1 tbsp (6 g) chopped mint

Salt and pepper, to taste

MINGLING MOJITO SAUCE
½ cup (120 ml) white rum

2 tbsp (30 ml) honey

¼ cup (60 ml) freshly squeezed lime juice

1 tbsp (6 g) chopped mint

1 tsp smoked paprika

Salt and pepper, to taste

FOR SERVING
2 tbsp (2 g) chopped cilantro

Lime wedges

Leftover Mingling Mojito Sauce

Ranch dressing (optional)

With a paper towel, pat the wings dry. Place the wings in a shallow dish or resealable plastic bag. Prepare the marinade. In a medium bowl, whisk together the rum, lime juice, orange juice, garlic, onion powder, brown sugar, crushed red pepper flakes, mint, salt and pepper. Pour the marinade over the wings and toss to coat. Cover and refrigerate for a minimum of 2 hours or overnight (the longer the better for best flavor results).

Preheat the grill or smoker to 350°F (180°C), indirect heat.

Grill the wings for 40 minutes or until they reach a minimum internal temperature of 165°F (75°C), or 190°F (90°C) if you like them well done, flipping them halfway through the cooking time. To crisp the skin, move the wings to the direct heat side of the grill, turning occasionally, until the skin is dark golden or to your liking.

Meanwhile, prepare the sauce. In a small saucepan over medium heat, whisk together the rum, honey, lime juice, mint, smoked paprika, salt and pepper. Bring to a boil and turn down the heat to low. Simmer for 10 to 15 minutes until the sauce has thickened, stirring occasionally.

Transfer the wings to a bowl and toss with Mingling Mojito Sauce until completely coated. Place the wings back on the grill grates for 5 to 10 minutes, until the sauce settles, or serve immediately. Plate and garnish them with cilantro. Serve them with lime wedges, leftover sauce and/or ranch dressing for dipping.

*See image on page 184 (shown on the bottom right).

SALTED CARAMEL WHISKEY

Salted caramel is not just for desserts. Let me introduce you to these addictive Salted Caramel Whiskey chicken wings that will blow your mind! They're sweet, salty, spicy and sticky-icky-icky in a beautiful golden caramel sauce. This is a whole new meaning to you can have your cake and eat it too, literally in wing form. Don't be skeptical; give these a try–you'll be pleasantly surprised.

SERVINGS: 4

2 lb (907 g) chicken wings, tips removed, drums and flats separated

MARINADE
½ cup (120 ml) Jack Daniel's® Tennessee Whiskey, or your favorite

2 tsp (10 g) brown sugar

1 tsp crushed red pepper flakes

2 tbsp (14 g) your favorite BBQ rub

Salt and pepper, to taste

SALTED CARAMEL SAUCE
1¼ cups (300 ml) dulce de leche (caramel sauce)

½ cup (120 ml) Jack Daniel's Tennessee Whiskey

½ tsp salt

¼ cup (60 ml) Frank's RedHot Original

2 tbsp (30 ml) low-sodium soy sauce

1 tbsp (14 g) brown sugar

FOR SERVING
Sea salt

Leftover Salted Caramel Sauce

Ranch dressing (optional)

Carrot and celery sticks

With a paper towel, pat the wings dry. Place the wings in a shallow dish or resealable plastic bag. Make the marinade. In a medium bowl, whisk together the whiskey, brown sugar, crushed red pepper flakes, BBQ rub, salt and pepper. Pour the marinade over the wings and toss to coat. Cover and refrigerate for a minimum of 2 hours or overnight (the longer the better for best flavor results).

Preheat the grill or smoker to 350°F (180°C), indirect heat.

Grill the wings for 40 minutes or until they reach a minimum internal temperature of 165°F (75°C), or 190°F (90°C) if you like them well done, flipping them halfway through the cooking time. To crisp the skin, move the wings to the direct heat side of the grill, turning occasionally, until the skin is dark golden or to your liking.

Meanwhile, prepare the sauce. In a large saucepan over medium heat, whisk together the dulce de leche, whiskey, salt, hot sauce and soy sauce. Bring to a boil, stirring frequently, and reduce the heat to low. Simmer for about 15 minutes, then add the brown sugar. Whisk until evenly mixed and simmer for an additional 5 minutes. The longer you simmer the thicker the sauce will become. Add more whiskey or water if the sauce is too thick for your liking.

Transfer the wings to a bowl and toss with the Salted Caramel Sauce until completely coated. Garnish them with sea salt and serve them with leftover sauce and/or ranch dressing for dipping and carrot and celery sticks.

*See image on page 184 (shown on the bottom left).

JACK AND COKE®

Does it get any better than BBQ, whiskey and chicken wings grilled to perfection? This classic combo will bring all the neighbors to your yard. These chicken wings are smothered in a sticky, lip-smacking sauce with whiskey, Coca-Cola, sriracha and brown sugar. Bring the napkins and a side of whiskey.

SERVINGS: 4

2 lb (907 g) chicken wings, tips removed, drums and flats separated

1 tsp paprika

1/8 tsp cayenne pepper

1/4 tsp chili powder

2 tsp (10 g) brown sugar

1 tsp garlic powder

1 tsp onion powder

Salt and pepper, to taste

JACK AND COKE SAUCE

1/2 cup (120 ml) Jack Daniel's Tennessee Whiskey

1/4 cup (60 ml) sriracha, or to taste

1/2 cup (120 ml) Coca-Cola

2 tbsp (28 g) brown sugar

2 tbsp (30 ml) low-sodium soy sauce

Salt and pepper, to taste

2 cloves garlic, minced

FOR SERVING

2 tbsp (12 g) chopped green onion

Ranch or blue cheese dressing

Carrot and celery sticks

With a paper towel, pat the wings dry. In a small bowl, combine the paprika, cayenne, chili powder, brown sugar, garlic powder, onion powder, salt and pepper. Sprinkle the prepared rub over the wings, coating evenly.

Preheat the grill or smoker to 350°F (180°C), indirect heat.

Grill the wings for 40 minutes or until they reach a minimum internal temperature of 165°F (75°C), or 190°F (90°C) if you like them well done, flipping them halfway through the cooking time. To crisp the skin, move the wings to the direct heat side of the grill, turning occasionally, until the skin is dark golden or to your liking.

Meanwhile, prepare the sauce. In a large saucepan over medium heat, whisk together the whiskey, sriracha, Coca-Cola, brown sugar, soy sauce, salt and pepper. Bring to a boil, stirring occasionally and add the garlic. Reduce the heat to low and simmer for 15 to 20 minutes or until the sauce thickens, stirring frequently.

Transfer the wings to a bowl and toss them with the Jack and Coke Sauce until completely coated. Place the wings back on the grill grates for 5 to 10 minutes, until the sauce settles, or serve immediately. Plate the wings and garnish them with green onion. Serve them with ranch or blue cheese dressing for dipping and carrot and celery sticks.

HENNESSY® HONEY

Henny wings? Yes! This recipe is all about the sauce. These chicken wings have a beautiful golden-brown finish, and are sticky to the touch and irresistibly delicious. This sauce is great to prepare ahead of time and warm up before tossing the wings.

SERVINGS: 4

2 lb (907 g) chicken wings, tips removed, drums and flats separated

1 tsp smoked paprika

1 tsp brown sugar

1 tsp garlic powder

1 tsp onion powder

1 tsp ginger powder

1/4 tsp chili powder

1/8 tsp cayenne pepper

1 tsp cornstarch

Salt and pepper, to taste

HENNESSY-HONEY SAUCE

1/4 cup (60 ml) ketchup

1/4 cup (60 ml) Frank's RedHot Original

2 tbsp (30 ml) apple cider vinegar

1/4–1/2 cup (60–120 ml) honey

1/2 cup (120 ml) Hennessy

1 tsp low-sodium soy sauce

1 tsp smoked paprika

1 tsp garlic powder

Salt and pepper, to taste

FOR SERVING

2 tbsp (12 g) chopped green onion

Leftover Hennessy-Honey Sauce

Ranch dressing (optional)

Carrot and celery sticks

With a paper towel, pat the wings dry. In a small bowl, combine the smoked paprika, brown sugar, garlic powder, onion powder, ginger powder, chili powder, cayenne, cornstarch, salt and pepper. Sprinkle the prepared rub over the wings, coating evenly.

Preheat the grill or smoker to 350°F (180°C), indirect heat.

Grill the wings for 40 minutes or until they reach a minimum internal temperature of 165°F (75°C), or 190°F (90°C) if you like them well done, flipping them halfway through the cooking time. To crisp the skin, move the wings to the direct heat side of the grill, turning occasionally until the skin is dark golden or to your liking.

Meanwhile, prepare the sauce. In a large saucepan over medium heat, whisk together the ketchup, hot sauce, apple cider vinegar, honey, Hennessy, soy sauce, smoked paprika, garlic powder, salt and pepper. Bring to a boil, stirring occasionally. Reduce the heat to low and simmer for about 5 minutes or until the sauce reduces and thickens, stirring frequently.

Transfer the wings to a bowl and toss with Hennessy-Honey Sauce until completely coated.

Place the wings back on the grill grates for 5 to 10 minutes, until the sauce settles, or serve immediately. Plate the wings and garnish them with green onion. Serve them with leftover sauce and/or ranch dressing for dipping and carrot and celery sticks.

*See image on page 189 (shown on the bottom right).

TEQUILA SUNRISE

A classic cocktail in the form of chicken wings—yum. The marinade infuses all those flavors, and the cherry-red hue looks like a sunrise. It's a perfect blend of flavor, color and tequila, plus it's paired with an incredible dipping sauce. These are sure to be a crowd-pleaser and perfect as an appetizer or a quick snack. Happy hour never tasted so good!

SERVINGS: 4

2 lb (907 g) chicken wings, tips removed, drums and flats separated

½ cup (120 ml) orange juice

⅓ cup (80 ml) tequila

¼ cup (60 ml) maraschino cherry juice or grenadine

½ tsp crushed red pepper flakes

1 tsp garlic powder

1 tsp smoked paprika

1 tbsp (15 ml) honey

Salt and pepper, to taste

SUNRISE DIPPING SAUCE

¼ cup (60 ml) ranch dressing

½ tsp maraschino cherry juice

½ tsp smoked paprika

½ tsp sriracha, or to taste

FOR SERVING

2 tbsp (12 g) chopped green onion

Orange slices

Maraschino cherries

Sunrise Dipping Sauce

With a paper towel, pat the wings dry. Place the wings in a shallow dish or resealable plastic bag. In a medium bowl, whisk together the orange juice, tequila, maraschino cherry juice, crushed red pepper flakes, garlic powder, smoked paprika, honey, salt and pepper. Pour the marinade over the wings and toss to coat. Cover and refrigerate for 4 hours or overnight (the longer the better for best flavor results).

Preheat the grill or smoker to 350°F (180°C), indirect heat.

Grill the wings for 40 minutes or until they reach a minimum internal temperature of 165°F (75°C), or 190°F (90°C) if you like them well done, flipping them halfway through the cooking time. To crisp the skin, move the wings to the direct heat side of the grill, turning occasionally, until the skin is dark golden or to your liking.

Meanwhile, prepare the dipping sauce. In a small bowl, combine the ranch dressing, maraschino cherry juice, smoked paprika and sriracha.

Plate the wings and garnish them with green onion. Serve them with orange slices, maraschino cherries and Sunrise Dipping Sauce.

*See image on page 189 (shown on the bottom left).

VODKA GUMMY BEAR

Gummy Bear chicken wings! Yes, melted candy sauce, it's a thing. Delicious, fruity gummy bears are soaked in vodka and melted down to a sticky, sweet and beautiful BBQ wing glaze. These are going to get the party started and will be the talk of the event. Substitute vodka for pineapple juice to make these alcohol-free.

SERVINGS: 4

GUMMY BEAR BBQ SAUCE

1 cup (120 g) gummy bears (all colors except the green ones)

Vodka

2 tbsp (30 ml) your favorite BBQ sauce

2 tbsp (30 ml) low-sodium soy sauce

Hot sauce, to taste

Water to thin out

2 lb (907 g) chicken wings, tips removed, drums and flats separated

1 tsp smoked paprika

1 tsp brown sugar

¼ tsp chili powder

1 tsp onion powder

1 tsp garlic powder

⅛ tsp cayenne pepper

Salt and pepper, to taste

FOR SERVING

Leftover Gummy Bear BBQ Sauce

Ranch dressing (optional)

Place the gummy bears in a mason jar or airtight container and pour in enough vodka to cover. Cover and refrigerate overnight.

With a paper towel, pat the wings dry. In a small bowl, combine the smoked paprika, brown sugar, chili powder, onion powder, garlic powder, cayenne, salt and pepper. Sprinkle the prepared rub over the wings, coating evenly.

Preheat the grill or smoker to 350°F (180°C), indirect heat.

Grill the wings for 40 minutes or until they reach a minimum internal temperature of 165°F (75°C), or 190°F (90°C) if you like them well done, flipping them halfway through the cooking time. To crisp the skin, move the wings to the direct heat side of the grill, turning occasionally, until the skin is dark golden or to your liking.

Meanwhile, prepare the sauce. In a small saucepan over medium heat, melt the gummy bears in vodka, 5 to 10 minutes, stirring frequently. Next, stir in the BBQ sauce, soy sauce and hot sauce. Reduce the heat to low and simmer for 10 to 15 minutes, stirring frequently. Add water if the sauce is too thick for your liking. Once the sauce cools, it will thicken up.

Transfer the wings to a bowl and toss with the Gummy Bear BBQ Sauce until completely coated. Place the wings back on the grill grates for 5 to 10 minutes, until the sauce settles, or serve immediately. Plate the wings and serve them with leftover sauce and/or ranch dressing for dipping.

ACKNOWLEDGMENTS

To my husband, best friend and taste tester. There aren't enough words to express my gratitude. Thank you for your support, patience and encouragement. This book would not have been possible without you. Thank you for always being by my side.

To Sandy, my late great grill sidekick dog. You were here for the start of this book but didn't stick around until I finished. She was always by my side when I was grilling, especially chicken wings. She brought tremendous joy into my life with her sassy personality. Also known as Gremlin, she was mischievous, adorable and grunted when hungry.

To my family, thank you from the bottom of my heart for the constant support, encouragement, love, inspiration and for fueling my passion from a young age. I would not be here or the person I am today without you. This book would not have been possible without you either.

To my friends, thank you for being a big part of this book with your constant support, encouragement and words of wisdom. I am grateful to have such amazing people in my life.

Thank you to the whole team at Louisiana Grills and Dansons for putting your faith in me, the constant support and the opportunity you have given me.

Thank you to Pitmasters Choice Pellets for providing the fuel to grill and for your support.

Thank you to Caitlin, Will and the whole team at Page Street Publishing for making my dream a reality and making this whole process smooth and enjoyable. I couldn't have asked for a better group of people.

To all my followers and my BBQ family, thank you for your constant love, support, inspiration, kind words and encouragement. I am grateful for the friendships I have made along the way. It means more to me than you'll ever know.

ABOUT THE AUTHOR

PAULA STACHYRA is a grill enthusiast, recipe developer, social influencer, photographer, content creator and backyard BBQ chef from Ontario, Canada. You'll always find her at her grill, even in the winter months, creating innovative, fun, simple and flavorful dishes. She loves to share her grill recipes, videos, tips and tricks to encourage more people to get outside and grill. Grilling started off as a hobby but has quickly become her passion. She's spreading the BBQ love one dish at a time as a Louisiana Grills team member.

Paula has had recipes featured by *Rachael Ray In Season* magazine's Instagram page, French's® brand mustard, Tabasco, Thrillist, Taste This Next, Surf No Turf and many more. She's been seen on live television grilling some of her favorite cheeseburger recipes for National Cheeseburger day. She has worked with some national brands such as Masterbuilt® grills, National Pork Board and many more.

INDEX